Social networking and contact

How social workers can help adoptive families

Eileen Fursland

Published by
British Association for Adoption & Fostering
(BAAF)
Saffron House
6-10 Kirby Street
London EC1N 8TS
www.baaf.org.uk

Charity registration 275689 (England and Wales) and SC039337 (Scotland)

© Eileen Fursland 2010

British Library Cataloguing in Publication Data
A catalogue record for this book is available from the British Library

ISBN 978 1 905664 97 9

Project management by Shaila Shah, Director of Publications, BAAF

Photograph on cover posed by models, by Sharon Aldridge-Bent

Designed and typeset by Helen Joubert Design

Printed in Great Britain by The Lavenham Press
Trade distribution by Turnaround Publisher Services, Unit 3, Olympia Trading Estate,
Coburg Road, London N22 6TZ

BAAF is the leading UK-wide membership organisation for all those concerned with
adoption, fostering and child care issues.

Contents

How this book came about

When BAAF first commissioned me to write about the impact of social networking on adoption, in late 2009, the plan was for three "pamphlets" on social networking websites and their role in contact issues with regard to adoption and fostering.

Shaila Shah, BAAF's Director of Publications, had realised that both parents and professionals, as well as adopted children and young people themselves, needed some information and advice on this issue.

Six months on, the "pamphlets" have turned into books – *Facing up to Facebook: A survival guide for adoptive families*, and *Social Networking and Contact: How social workers can help adoptive families*.

Why the transformation? Shaila and I quickly realised that pamphlets alone would not be enough to meet the huge need for information and advice on this issue. From the very beginning of my research, it became clear that social networking was having a huge impact on adoptive families and adoption professionals alike. I sent out an email to adoption social workers, via BAAF's network, which was circulated widely – I had a huge response, even receiving email replies from the United States and Australia. Social workers reported a steady stream of cases. The overriding message I received was: 'Thank goodness this is being addressed. I have no answers but I hope someone does.' One social worker said: 'I feel as though my role so far has been to run along behind with a mop.'

Adoption UK has a messageboard for adoptive parents. Messages posted there make clear the level of concern among parents about the risks of social networking for their adopted children. Adoption UK posted a request from me on its messageboard asking adoptive families to contact me if they had been affected by this issue. The parents who contacted me know, more than anyone, how important it is for adopted children and young people that we get this right.

My research showed that many adoptive families have concerns and some are struggling with the emotional consequences of situations thrown up by the use of social networking sites. Adoption professionals are facing completely new challenges and having to help and support families who find themselves in situations they never imagined. Many authorities have not yet developed guidelines and social workers are having to find ways of managing this complex issue as it affects more and more families.

BAAF quickly responded – Shaila agreed that instead of pamphlets we would publish two comprehensive books. BAAF arranged a conference to bring together IT and other professionals to discuss the issue. A third book – this time for foster carers, who are faced with different issues – is currently in production; a publication for young people will follow. Following on from the conference, BAAF hopes to run workshops for social workers and also publish a training pack, which can be used to deliver training in this issue to practitioners. BAAF's books, conference and training are timely and have been eagerly awaited.

The experiences of adoption practitioners and adoptive families inform every page of this book. If the book doesn't always provide neat answers, that's because it's rooted in real life, which can be messy. The many responses I received, the questions I was asked and everything I heard and read during the course of my research for this book showed me that this issue is of urgent relevance to everyone involved in adoption.

Note: Please note that I have alternated the use of "he" and "she" throughout. For example, in Part 1, I use "He", in Part 2 "She", and then in Part 3, "He" again. All references, of course, apply to both sexes. Please note also that, where names have been used in case examples, these have all been changed to protect confidentiality.

Acknowledgements

I would like to thank the social workers who told me about their experiences, passed on what they had learned or observed, and suggested questions for the book to address. The social workers (I can't thank them individually as many did not wish to be named, but they know who they are!) work in local authority adoption services in Anglesey, Bedfordshire, Berkshire, Brighton & Hove, Bristol, Bury, Cardiff, Cumbria, Edinburgh, Halton, Leicester, London (boroughs of Camden, Islington, Southwark, Havering and Harrow), Leeds, Luton, Manchester, Neath, North Yorkshire, Nottingham, Pembrokeshire, Reading, Sheffield, Stockport and Southampton.

Thanks to the adoptive parents who shared their experiences, wisdom and hard-won insights in the hope that these will help others. They took on the most difficult job in the world – being a parent to someone else's child – before anyone had ever heard of Facebook. And for some of them, the revolution in social networking has had unforeseen consequences, demanding reserves of strength, courage, patience and understanding that they could never have anticipated when they first adopted their child. I am grateful to them and to Adoption UK for offering to post my request.

Professionals from voluntary adoption agencies and other organisations also offered valuable input, including: Action for Children; Adoption UK; Child and Family Court Advisory and Support Service; Child Exploitation and Online Protection Service (CEOPS); Fever PR (for Facebook); Norwood; Our Place, Bristol; the Post-Adoption Centre, London; and Soldiers, Sailors, Airmen and Families Association.

Thanks are due to the following people for their help:

Lynda Gilbert, Adoption UK
Kate Richardson, CEOPS
Keitha Wakefield, Development Co-ordinator; and the North-East London Adoption Group
Norma Sargent, Coram Adoption Service
Susan Grindon, Assistant Team Manager; and the Post Adoption Team, Surrey County Council

I would also like to thank Alison Vincent (Adoption Consultant, Berkshire Adoption Advisory Service), Catherine Grace (Cabrini Children's Society) and Julia Venables

(Adoption Team, Essex County Council) for the discussions on this issue; and Alison, Catherine and Catherine Sturrock (Social Workers, Post Adoption Team, Essex County Council) for reading and commenting on the draft.

Thank you to everyone at BAAF who contributed to the book in any way:

Shaila Shah, Director of Publications, who originated the idea and commissioned the books.

Jo Francis, Editor, for preparing the scripts.

John Simmonds, Director of Policy, Research and Development and Elaine Dibben, Adoption Consultant, for reading and commenting on the drafts and for their many helpful suggestions.

John Simmonds, for contributing the Foreword.

Alexandra Conroy-Harris (Legal Consultant), Julia Feast (Policy, Research & Development Consultant), Katrina Wilson (Information Officer) and Lindsey Dunbar (Trainer, North-west Region), BAAF, for their expertise and input.

Eileen Fursland

Note about the author

Eileen Fursland is a freelance writer. She writes mainly about social issues, particularly those affecting children. Eileen has contributed many articles to a range of magazines and newspapers, including *The Guardian*. She has written three books: *Children's Play*; *Working Mum's Handbook* (with Carole Smillie); and *Get Your Kids Fit!* (with Kelly Holmes), all published by Virgin Publishing; and an online reference source for anyone who works with children and young people, called *Understanding the Child* (to be published by Pearson Publishing Group in September 2010).

For BAAF, Eileen has authored or co-authored a number of books, guides and booklets, including *Caring for a Young Person who has been Trafficked: A guide for foster carers*, and a series of booklets on caring for unaccompanied asylum-seeking children and young people. She has written a series of training programmes with Kate Cairns (*Trauma and Recovery*; *Safer Caring*; *Transitions and Endings*; and *Building Identity*) as well as *Preparing to Adopt: A training pack for preparation groups* (with a BAAF working party).

Her most recent publications for BAAF are this book and a guide for adoptive families called *Facing up to Facebook: A survival guide for adoptive families*.

Foreword

Adoption has always been in a state of evolution and change. We have seen the nature of adoption radically change over the last 50 years from one which provided a solution to society's negative attitudes to illegitimacy and single parenthood and unavailability of effective contraception and legal abortion to one which provides a solution to serious issues arising from child maltreatment and parental risk and breakdown. Although both sets of circumstances focus on the child's lifelong need for a family, in which they are loved and belong, the circumstances in which the child is placed and the implications of this in the long term are now quite different. This is markedly so where the child is removed from his or her parents through legal proceedings instituted by the State and against the wishes of those parents, but even where consent is obtained, the actuality or likelihood of significant risk or harm to the child is likely to have played some part. However, although this is so in the UK, it is unlikely to be so in many other countries where by far the greater number of adoptions are likely to be intercountry adoptions. The exception to this is the USA, where maltreated children placed for adoption, intercountry adoption and children relinquished by their parents exist alongside each other and which therefore presents a more complex picture.

As adoption has changed, so has the view that it was best kept a secret because it was a new start in life, and that what went before was an unnecessary complexity in the child's view of who they were and what they were to become. While for some families secrecy was never an acceptable idea, others were confused and disturbed by what was recommended, and for yet others, it was something that they adhered to, with the adoption being disclosed to the child only much later or very late in life. But this then accepted view was challenged through the 1960s and 70s and families were advised that children should be told and the story of their adoption incorporated in a meaningful and sensitive way into family history and narrative. This then started to include forms of contact – for some, confined to periodic exchanges of information; for others, more open forms of communication including direct contact. For adults, the process was facilitated by the opening and availability of adoption records and support being available to find and make contact with birth parents and relatives. Similar opportunities were afforded to birth parents themselves. The complexity and emotion that such opportunities brought about were exquisitely demonstrated in Mike Leigh's film *Secrets and Lies*. Research by Feast, Howe and Triseliotis presented a more comprehensive evidence-based picture.

Such developments were not easily achieved and at the time there were fears that, if records were opened, there was potential for risk, particularly if adopted individuals were angry with birth parents about being given up for adoption. This fear was never realised in practice. Accompanying these developments was the recognition of just how significant children's curiosity about their adoption actually was and how enduring that could be. Commonly-asked questions included: Why was I adopted? Was there something about me that made my birth parents give me up? Was I unlovable?, accompanied by others such as: Who are my birth parents? What do they look like? Would they love me more than you do? Not every child asked these questions and of course they were many other questions too. For some, the intensity of their curiosity never diminished. It may have been something that they kept to themselves or it may have been shared with a friend or with adoptive parents or other family members. For others, it may have come and gone and returned again at different points in their development and particularly in adolescence, or was something of little significance.

The part that indirect and direct forms of contact have played in the evolution of adoption has been highly significant. Ensuring that these arrangements between adoptive families and birth families are safe and in the child's best interests has rested in the mediating role of the adoption agency. If identifying information was to be withheld, then that would be the responsibility of the adoption agency and managed by them. If information was to be exchanged, then that would need to happen through the adoption agency. If there were changes of circumstances and a request to change arrangements, then this would be mediated by the adoption agency. This is not to say that adoptive families and birth families didn't or don't make these arrangements themselves directly without going through the adoption agency – some do, although we know little about this. But the role of the adoption agency in managing, mediating and arranging links between adoptive families and birth families cannot be underestimated. And this has become even more pronounced as adoption has come to involve children who have been maltreated. The management of risk, keeping the child safe, and maintaining the integrity and functioning of the adoptive family are continuing responsibilities of the agency. That is not to say that all birth parents continue to pose a risk – many certainly do not. But the agency always has a responsibility to ensure, wherever it can, that confidentiality of identifying information is maintained and the nature, frequency and amount of information exchanged is manageable for the child and adopters. These issues change over time in individual cases and sometimes in unplanned or unpredictable ways, but the agency has a primary responsibility to ensure that the placement is secure and the child's needs met.

And then we have the advent of social networking sites; prominent among them all is Facebook. Social networking allows people to exchange information with little effort, find people they have lost contact with, and establish new "friends" in ways that were previously unthought of. It has had a significant impact on the notion of social identity, personal relating and relationships and privacy. It has provided new ways for people to communicate but it has posed risks to privacy and provided new opportunities for exploitation of the vulnerable.

It is clear that many of these issues have impacted on adoption. They have developed fairly rapidly as social networking has developed rapidly, but recently the issues have suddenly gathered momentum and it is now clear that many people – adopted children and their adoptive parents, birth parents and other birth family members – and adoption agencies have been profoundly affected by the ease, directness and opportunities social networking sites make available. Social networking allows individuals to circumvent the agency's established role in preserving confidentiality, mediating information exchange and providing guidance and support. It has resulted in breaches of confidentiality and unexpected, unplanned and unthought-through contact resulting in distress, anxiety and unsettled young people and adoptive parents. It is a serious and worrying development. There are also examples where it has provided opportunity for the exchange of information in constructive, helpful and enriching ways.

What is clear is that something significant has changed about adoption through the advent of social networking and there is no going back on this. Some of the discussion that has occurred suggests that adoption needs to fundamentally change. Other people believe that, as adoption has always done, it needs to adapt. What is clear is that there is no question that any adoptive family, birth family or adoption agency can ignore social networking. Policy and practice will need to develop to ensure that all the advantages that adoption brings continue to be available to those children who need it. It should not and must not be undermined by social networking.

Eileen Fursland has been the first to explore the nature of people's experience of the impact of social networking sites in adoption and, in gathering that information together, has identified a number of important issues that are likely to inform adoption practice in years to come. What started out as a brief by BAAF to write guidance turned into a major journey of discovery. Eileen was told about many experiences involving social networking that have affected adopted young people and their families and birth relatives. Sometimes the lessons to be learned are clear; sometimes questions remain. Some of the experiences told to Eileen were disturbing and upsetting, others indicated where important lessons had been learnt. Eileen has pulled all of this together in an important guide that is groundbreaking in its significance. There is no doubt that there is more to be learnt as the issues evolve, but there couldn't be a firmer ground on which to do so.

John Simmonds
Director of Policy, Research and Development, BAAF

May 2010

Adoption and social networking

Adoption social workers, adoptive parents, adopted children and adults and birth families are all facing an unprecedented situation. The revolution in social networking on the internet - and, in particular, Facebook - has made it easier than ever before to trace people.

Increasing numbers of young people who were adopted as babies or young children are now searching for their birth families without realising the complexity of what they are doing or where it could lead. And there are instances, too, where birth relatives are tracing their children and approaching them via the internet.

Some adopted adolescents - often volatile and vulnerable - are secretly having direct contact with and even meeting up with birth parents and siblings without their adoptive parents' knowledge. They are renewing relationships with parents, siblings and extended family members, often leading to tangled and difficult situations affecting several families.

Tracing and reunion can be emotional dynamite. Going through Facebook circumvents all the careful processes put in place to prepare, protect and support everyone involved in adoption contact and reunion. It takes away the safety net of going through an intermediary. And it moves quickly - sometimes too quickly. It often falls to social workers to help everyone involved to manage the risks and to cope with the fallout.

Here's an example of just how challenging these situations can become.

CASE STUDY

Alison and Mike have two adopted daughters aged 16 and 10 and a birth son aged four. The adoption was seven years ago. One day, Alison discovers that the eldest, Emma, has traced her birth mother and birth father on Facebook and has been emailing and texting them for three weeks. Both were drug-takers and the father was violent. Emma's Facebook page contains some information - her school and the town where she lives - that could lead to the parents tracing her.

Emma is hostile to Alison and Mike and refuses to listen when they try to explain the possible risks of inviting her birth parents into her life (and the implications for her younger sister). She seems to have forgotten her parents' drug-taking and violence - she is excited about talking to them and the fact that they are telling her they love her and miss her. When Alison and Mike try to talk to her about it, she flies into a rage and accuses them of trying to stop her from contacting her birth parents.

Alison and Mike understand that Emma now needs to have contact with her birth parents but they want it to be in a safe setting, done through social services and with support for Emma. But Emma won't listen.

There is no way of stopping her from accessing the internet – if they tried, they know she would just use a computer at a friend's house. They feel that if they try too hard to control things, they will simply push her closer to her birth parents. They don't know what to do and are desperately worried that Emma might run away or that the birth father might turn up on their doorstep.

Facebook can be a force for good, of course – it just depends on how people use it. For instance, social networking, emailing and sharing photographs online or talking to each other via a webcam can be invaluable ways for family members to keep in touch with each other. With the internet, even when people are geographically far apart, they can keep in touch and maintain a relationship which may not be possible face to face. When online contact has been planned and agreed, it can be helpful in adoption and fostering.

And sometimes, even when a child initiates contact through Facebook, this can work out well in the longer term, as in the case below and other examples given in this book.

> *An adopted girl aged 15 was cajoled by friends into making contact with her birth mother on Facebook. She went on to meet up with her birth mother. This was initially very upsetting for the adoptive family. But I have been working with the family for over a year now and things have settled down considerably and developed into a regular pattern.*
>
> AN ADOPTION SOCIAL WORKER

As a result of social networking, the fundamental principles that have been taken for granted in adoption are now being called into question:

- Where does it leave contact agreements, now that a few minutes in front of a computer could one day put birth parents and their child back in direct, unmediated contact with each other?

- In future, how many birth parents will wait until their child is 18 and then request the chance to contact him through an intermediary service, rather than trying to find him on Facebook?

- What are the implications for some of the accepted practices in adoption which could, now, make it easier for adopted children and their families to trace each other? There are a number of these, from retaining the child's first name (if it is an unusual name) to including his birth certificate in his life story book.

This book looks at some of the pressing questions facing adoption practitioners.

- Adopted children, adoptive families and birth families need additional information, input and support on these issues. How can social workers ensure that they can provide this?

- Which, if any, aspects of policy and practice need to change to reflect the new situation?

- How can children's and young people's privacy be protected?

- What - if anything - can be done about unauthorised and unmediated contact?

- What do social workers themselves need to know about the internet, Facebook and other social networking sites and protecting privacy and security online?

Although it is too early to produce many definitive answers on this issue, some general principles apply. As in all social work practice, it is important to consider the individual situation in every case, make well informed assessments of risks and how they can be moderated, draw on our knowledge and experience of other dilemmas in adoption and ensure that support is available to all parties involved.

The book has three main themes:

- Part 1: What do prospective adopters, adopted children, adoptive families and birth families need to know about adoption in the Facebook age? And how can we equip them for the new challenges?

- Part 2: What do social workers need to know about social networking and protecting privacy on the internet so that they can give good advice to adopted children and young people and their families?

- Part 3: How are social workers managing the complex situations that arise from direct, unmediated contact between adopted young people and their birth families?

The experiences of adoption practitioners and adoptive families on the front line inform every page of this book. This guide attempts to set out where we are now. It doesn't always provide neat answers and that's because it's rooted in real life. But it does raise important questions and offers a lot of information and advice on managing contact in the age of social networking.

How can we equip all parties for the new challenges?

Pre-adoption

Adoption preparation courses

No preparation course should now duck the issue of Facebook and other social networking sites and their potential for facilitating contact.

At open evenings for prospective adopters, discuss the issue of contact in general terms. Be prepared to answer questions honestly but, if possible, without scaring people away.

In training groups and preparation courses, the discussion can go into more detail about the reasons for confidentiality, as well as the likelihood of contact, and look at the challenges posed by the internet and social networking in particular.

Adopters need to make an informed decision about adoption and everything it is likely to entail. And in the age of Facebook, this means taking on board that it is possible there will be direct contact with their child's birth parents when he becomes a teenager or sometimes even earlier.

> *My view is that adoption is going to have to become more open in order to cope with the risks to confidentiality that arise from the internet and social networking, i.e. practice has to change to reflect the times, rather than thinking we can somehow manage and restrict children's access to the web in the long term or (as some have advocated!) not giving them enough information about their backgrounds to enable them to run a search for names on Facebook – basically, taking away their life story books and background letters!*
>
> AN ADOPTION SUPPORT SOCIAL WORKER

Stress the need to be open with the child

It's now widely accepted practice, informed by research, that adopted children need information about their family origins and that they benefit from openness rather than secrecy around their adoption and birth family. With the increasing possibility that children will decide to look for answers on the internet or perhaps be approached online by a birth relative, openness has become more important than ever.

Adopted children can sometimes fantasise about their birth relatives and idealise them when they are not given any information. They need to know the truth about their birth family, even if this is unpalatable or painful. Many adoption social workers believe that, if parents have always been open with the child, there's a greater chance that he will ask them when he wants more information.

Preparation sessions explain life story work to adopters and the need to give a child information about their history in an age-appropriate way. Trainers should emphasise that this doesn't just apply to early and later childhood, but throughout adolescence and beyond. Telling a child or young person about his story is not a one-off event, but needs to be an open and ongoing communication with him that responds to his need to know and his level of understanding.

Researchers David Brodzinsky and colleagues (1998) have outlined a psychosocial model of adoption adjustment, looking at the developmental tasks that face adopted people throughout their lifetime.

The main adoption-related psychosocial tasks in adolescence are seen as:

- further exploration of the meaning and implications of adoption;
- connecting adoption to one's sense of identity; tend to guard thoughts;
- coping with ethnic identity in cases of transracial adoption;
- coping with physical differences from family members;
- resolving family romance fantasy; want more information about birth parents;
- coping with adoption-related loss, especially as it relates to the sense of self;
- considering the possibility of searching for biological family.

It's important for adoptive parents not to avoid the subject of the child's birth family and not to give the impression that they would feel hurt, annoyed or rejected if he wanted to know more about his birth family. For instance, parents may share letterbox letters with their child and regularly talk about his adoption and his birth parents as well as sharing life story books or work that has been done with or for him.

Explore the issues for adopters who may need to outline potential risks to their vulnerable youngsters rather earlier than child development and understanding might dictate. Telling your child their birth parent was an abuser and may pose a threat is not easy at any age – when, how, with what support? How can the child still feel safe?

LYNDA GILBERT, POLICY CONSULTANT TO ADOPTION UK

Stress the long-term benefits of contact

Prospective adopters learn about the benefits of agreed contact, which can encompass different types of direct or letterbox communication between the child and his birth parents, siblings and sometimes other birth relatives.

In many cases, as time goes on, contact lapses. Perhaps the birth parents lead chaotic lives and stop collecting the letterbox letters. Sometimes adoptive parents find contact with birth parents harder than they thought they would, once they become attached to the child and start to think of him as theirs. They may also develop a deeper understanding of how their child has been damaged by his early life with his parents and this can make them feel ambivalent about writing with news about how the child is doing.

The child may not show much interest in either letters or face-to-face visits. Contact can be difficult to arrange or fit in with the family's other commitments, and adoptive parents sometimes may wonder why they are bothering.

> *With very young children it may seem to adopters that contact meetings are of little point or value to the child as he or she is not asking questions about adoption. What is likely to help such adopters persist with contact is an understanding that the child will need to address questions of identity in the future. In my research, adopters who showed a good understanding of the lifelong needs of their child were more highly motivated to sustain contact as they had long-term goals in mind.*
>
> NEIL, 2002

Stress to adopters that maintaining letterbox or direct contact, over the years, is more important than it may seem at the time and that sharing letterbox contact with the child does serve a purpose. It shows him that his adoptive parents expect him to be interested in his birth parents - and that he doesn't need to keep this a secret. All forms of contact maintain a link with the child's birth family, which may become vital later on in his life. It is something the adopters can build on if they need to. Making it a priority in the early years could save the family a lot of heartache later on.

Maintaining privacy

As outlined above, adoption preparation should stress the importance of open communication *with the child*. However, it should also include the need for care to protect information from people *outside the family*. From the start of the process, adopters need to know about precautions they should take to reduce the risk that their adopted child could be traced via the internet. (This is covered in detail in Part 2.)

Over 23 million people aged 13 and over in the UK are on Facebook, and the numbers are growing. And, Facebook aside, the possibilities for internet searching are becoming more sophisticated and powerful all the time. Young people and birth relatives can look for instant answers, online. It makes the adoption contact registers seem suddenly redundant.

Children's names

When a child is adopted, the child's new surname is meant to be kept secret. Sometimes, people inadvertently let this slip. Support should be provided to adopters and young people if the security of the placement has been put at risk. But even without the surname, there are possibilities for finding people on the internet and on social networking sites in particular. A determined person, who is prepared to put in the time, can piece together bits of information they know or have gleaned and an internet search can provide leads which they may be able to follow up.

Changing a child's first name

There are situations where adopters and professionals involved in adoption are wondering whether it is safer to change the child's first name as well as his surname to make it harder for birth relatives to trace him. This is a difficult question and one that arouses strong feelings. Social workers are aware that a child's first name is a vital part of his identity. But now that the internet has made tracing much easier, this raises questions about whether the need to protect a child's identity, when the birth family poses a threat, outweighs the arguments in favour of keeping his name, especially if it is an unusual one. There are examples of some adopters simply going ahead and changing the child's name anyway, even if they have agreed not to.

Adoption agencies are starting to develop risk assessment tools to help them in weighing up levels of risks and how these may impact on contact arrangements. Changing a child's first name is a significant decision which is likely to need addressing in a minority of cases where there are particular risks posed by the birth parents or the uniqueness of a child's given name. These decisions should be taken only after a full assessment of the issues. Sometimes, changing an unusual spelling to a more usual one might be all that is necessary.

It's also important to remember that, in many cases of Facebook contact, it is the young person who makes the contact – not the birth parent. So unless we are prepared to keep the child's name secret from him until he is 18, there are no guarantees that even changing the name would prevent direct contact.

Changing a child's surname

There is case law which makes it clear that adopters have to continue using the child's birth family surname until the adoption order has been granted. This means that, when he is first placed with them, they have to register him in school and with a doctor in his birth surname rather than the one he is going to have. Everyone – parents and health and education professionals alike – should take extra care during this period to keep his identity confidential, e.g. by not posting anything about him on the internet.

How could names lead a birth parent to the child?

- Even if they don't know the child's new surname, an unusual first name could be a way of tracing him.

- They may search the internet for the child, for instance, by using the child's two first names or the first name(s) in combination with any other information they know, such as his date of birth or the city he lives in.

- If two children were adopted together, the parent could carry out a search for the two names and find instances where those two names are mentioned together.

- If the child is good at a particular sport or musical instrument, for example, the parent may search for and find his name in sports reports or reports of performances or awards, particularly if they know the town or city he lives in.

- If the birth parents have met the adoptive parents and know their first names – particularly if these are distinctive – they may be able to search for both the parents' names and find instances where they appear together. They may also be able to search for the parents' names on social networking sites and recognise them from their profile photographs.

- If some information has been given pre-adoption or during face-to-face contact, such as the parents' first names and occupations, the birth parents may be able to search for information on the internet that could identify the adoptive family.

I think parents who use these sites need to keep in mind how easy it is to identify possible hits from very little information if you are prepared to put the time in.

AN ADOPTIVE PARENT

Parents should be careful what they put in their letterbox letters. If they write 'My son is in the Scouts and he is going to the World Jamboree this year,' only a few kids do that, so it could help the birth parent to piece things together.

AN ADOPTION SOCIAL WORKER

Social workers' duty to protect privacy

Social workers must ensure that they keep all adopters' information safe during the early stages of matching and beyond. A throwaway remark about an adopter's job or current location can lead to compromised security of the placement.

LYNDA GILBERT, POLICY CONSULTANT TO ADOPTION UK

The case outlined below shows how serious the consequences of "leaked" personal details can be for adoptive families.

CASE STUDY

M was placed for adoption with Mr and Mrs B and their older adopted child at the age of three. She had been removed from her birth parents following abuse, and her father had been convicted of physically abusing her, and of the manslaughter of her younger sibling. Between coming into care and being placed for adoption, M had been placed with her maternal grandmother and it was intended at the time of placement that there should be some future direct contact. Despite this, the adopters asked the local authority specifically to keep their address and the area in which they lived secret from the birth family and the local authority agreed. Inadvertently, however, at a matching meeting attended by the maternal grandmother, some of the social workers let slip the Bs' surname and the area where they lived. Shortly after M came to live with the Bs, the first of a series of incidents occurred which, in the eyes of the B family, amounted to a campaign of harassment. These incidents ranged from telephone calls, some silent, some threatening, to attacks on the Bs' car and the placing of a dead cat in the postbox outside their door with the words "You're next" sprayed on the door.

The Bs took the local authority to court for damages. The judge found that the local authority did have a duty of care in negligence to the Bs (i.e. had been negligent) but at the same time dismissed the family's claim because he considered they hadn't been able to prove that the birth family had been responsible. The Bs appealed, and the local authority appealed against the finding that it had been negligent. Both the appeals were dismissed.

> *The local authority had argued that, as a matter of public policy, the claim should not be allowed to succeed for fear it would discourage adoption agencies from pursuing "open" adoptions, in case they made themselves liable to action if the adopters' confidentiality were breached. But this argument was dismissed. The number of "open" adoptions, where potentially very serious consequences would flow from disclosure of the adopters' identity or whereabouts, was likely to be small. Each case would have to be considered on its own facts, but where, as here, the agency gave an explicit undertaking to maintain confidentiality, it would not in any way undermine the general system of adoption to require them to abide by their undertaking.*
>
> CULLEN, 2007

Safeguarding information during court proceedings

- Personal information about adopters is sometimes mistakenly revealed during court proceedings. Court staff and children's guardians may need training in the need to safeguard adopters' information.

- Social workers involved in child protection and care proceedings should address safeguarding issues through the final statement to the court.

- Thought should be given to adoption hearings being held in the area from where the child has been placed rather than where the adoptive parents live, so as not to provide information about where the child is located.

Contact

There should be a risk assessment on each case, with an in-depth consideration about the implications of contact. This should involve the children's team, legal team and Guardian.

Thought needs to be given to whether providing letterbox photographs is appropriate. (See below, and section on photographs in Part 2. See also Appendix 2, *An example of a risk assessment for the use of photographs in information exchange (letterbox) services.*)

Local authorities are now beginning to address whether contact agreements and information provided to birth parents from now on should explicitly address the issue of contact via social networking sites (making clear that this is not an acceptable way of making contact). However, contact agreements are voluntary and therefore difficult to enforce but things can be done to strengthen these agreements.

Contact agreements should be seen as a formal document, more like a contract, with specific consequences being spelt out. Breaches of the agreement should lead to a review of the letterbox or direct contact, involving work with all parties. All parties should sign the contact agreement – if everything is written down and they have agreed to it, people show that they have understood it and committed to it. It may also make it more difficult for them to "rewrite history" at a later date.

Where birth parents are believed to pose a serious risk, there may be a need to consider court orders in relation to contact when a child is being adopted.

There have been cases where the judge has put into the adoption order that any photographs given must not be shared or distributed, including on social networking sites – birth parents have had to sign agreements and would be in breach of a court order if they did not comply.

Be mindful of the issues when setting up direct contact and monitor letterbox carefully. Herein lies a minefield, especially where some siblings are in touch with birth family and others not. There is a move in favour of contact but without doing proper risk assessments, not just for infancy but beyond into growing independence. Often adopters are left to manage these arrangements downstream without advice and support. In my view, contact without support is highly risky.

LYNDA GILBERT, POLICY CONSULTANT TO ADOPTION UK

Support in the years ahead

Make sure prospective adopters are well informed about their entitlement to request an assessment for adoption support at any time in the future if problems arise. This includes mediation services in relation to contact between the adopted child and others, including birth parents and birth brothers and sisters.

Prospective adopters won't always take in all the messages they are given, pre-adoption. And of course, as the child gets older, he will want and need to know more – and parents may need help with this. At some stage he may want to re-open contact with his family. So agencies should try to re-address these issues in post-adoption training, if at all possible.

Adoptive parents need to understand that one day, when their child is much older, he may decide to read all the information from his adoption file, including their letters. At that particular time, he may be more inclined to see things from his birth parents' perspective. He might even be moved by the fact that his birth parents wanted to have contact with him.

Where there are approaches from birth parents about re-negotiating contact **before** a child becomes 18 – or 16 in Scotland – social workers and adoptive parents need to carefully consider whether to review or reopen current contact arrangements within the context of the law. If adoptive parents decide to refuse a particular request from the birth parents – e.g. for photographs or to be able to see the child – you could suggest they write down their reasons so that their child will have an explanation of why they made those decisions at that time.

Adopted children and young people

Their need to know

It is normal, natural and healthy for adopted children to be curious about their birth parents and their brothers and sisters, to wonder what they are like and even to wish they could meet them. Questions of "identity" come sharply into focus as children reach adolescence. Adolescents start to wonder about who they really are, what has shaped them and how others see them.

Adopted young people have more questions and experience more confusion than most. There is a natural urge to find out about their origins and fill in the gaps. This is why life story work cannot be left at the level that seemed to meet the child's needs when he was five or ten. Young people have different questions and want more information.

Even if they have been told everything about their past, they may still develop a strong need to know what is happening to their birth parents and/or brothers and sisters *now*.

> *I am aware of one case of a 14-year-old leaving her adoptive home and disappearing to live with her birth father (but in this case I know that the adopters did not respond a few years earlier when she had questions about her birth family, so it could have been curiosity getting the better of her)...Good communication between adopters and their child sounds obvious, but frankly I see cases of children unable to ask poignant questions as their development and understanding increase.*
>
> AN ADOPTION SOCIAL WORKER

For young people who were adopted, particularly if they suffered neglect or abuse in early life, the teenage years are often turbulent. Relationships with their adoptive family can become strained, sometimes to breaking point. Just like other teenagers, adopted teenagers test boundaries to the limit, appear to reject their parents, trigger huge family rows and feel like running away. But there is an added dimension to all of this for an adopted teenager. Somewhere out there is another parent or parents, even though little or nothing may be known of their current circumstances.

> *It was just so easy for our daughter to find her birth parents on Facebook – almost too tempting. It is so easy for children to get on these sites and look for people without really understanding the possible consequences for all involved. Adopted children often have multiple problems, and are often looking for "something else" in their lives, no matter how happy and loved they've been in their adoptive families. Finding their "other" family on Facebook can probably seem like the answer to some of them but will almost certainly cause them much heartache in the long run.*
>
> AN ADOPTIVE MOTHER

It can be important for an adopted child's self-esteem to know that his birth parents care and want to see him.

Children and young people with unmet needs are more likely to search for their birth family. Post-adoption training should try to get across to adoptive parents the message that, often, attempts to make contact arise out of a need to know more; and that they should do their best to tell the child (or help him find out) what he needs to know. But not all adoptive parents are keen to share information, as in the case below:

CASE STUDY

A few years ago an 11-year-old girl emailed adoption services, saying that she had been thinking about her birth mother and did not have any information about her and asked if we could send her some information. My manager emailed her back saying we would need to speak to her parents, which we did. Her adoptive parents were very surprised, saying they were open with her. They had received letterbox news from her birth father since her placement, but not the birth mother and her whereabouts were unknown.

Coincidentally, the birth mother contacted me only a few months later to say she was back in the area and asked for help to write a letter and send photos. I contacted the adoptive parents and they agreed. For the last few years we have sent on the birth mother's letters.

Last year I had reason to speak to the adoptive parents with a concern about contact, to be told that they had not shared any of the letters sent by the birth parents with their daughter, now aged nearly 16.

So, even when people say they are open, they are sometimes not, and sometimes they do not understand or want to understand that their children will be curious. I have to question what messages they have been given in their training.

An adoption social worker

Life story work

Local authorities are required by statutory guidance to include an adopted child's birth parents' first names and the birth family surname in the life story book, so this is standard practice. However, these and other details can allow the child to search for his parents online and possibly find out all sorts of things about them or send them a message.

For some parents and professionals, their anxieties have led them to feel that practice should change and the child's surname should be kept separately from the life story book rather than in it; then parents can gauge the best time to tell the child this. However, others feel that leaving the surname out of the life story book gives the wrong message and will simply make the child more curious about what else is being kept from him. They believe that doing this does not take account of the value to the child of knowing about his past. Again, any decisions about this need to be based on the specific details of the case and be proportionate to the risks presented.

It is important that the information in the life story book gives a clear and honest explanation, albeit in an age-appropriate way, of why the child was placed for adoption.

Social workers are also required to prepare a "later life letter" which the adoptive parents can give to their child when they feel the time is right or when the child wants more information. It should be given to the adoptive parents before the adoption order is made.

This is written by the child's social worker to the child, to be read when he is a young adult, to give him a fuller picture of his background and the reasons for his adoption. If the letter is written by the social worker who knew his parents, it is important to give a brief description of them. This letter will build on the simple version provided in the life story book, and answer more of the young person's questions. It is important to be truthful and to give a clear picture of why his birth parents could not care for him, but also to give these difficult events some context which helps to explain his parents' difficulties. It is helpful to end on a positive note and recall the time when the young person's adoptive parents first met him, and how delighted they were – giving confirmation of the young person's place as a member of the adoptive family.

KANIUK, 2010

Re-opening contact

Sometimes young people (either alone or with their adoptive parents) will ask for help from adoption support services in finding out current information about their birth family or even re-opening contact with them. Perhaps the agreed contact arrangements lapsed or perhaps contact was not allowed at the time the child was adopted. It's important for agencies to respond as quickly as possible to such requests – if the young person has decided to go through the "proper channels" rather than via Facebook, he should not have to wait too long for answers.

Sometimes adoptive families who have had successful indirect contact over a period of time are happy to make the contact direct, for instance, with phone calls and perhaps even face-to-face meetings. Emails, instant messaging and the use of social networking sites are also channels through which the adoptive and birth families or the child and his birth relative could have this kind of agreed contact.

We have been working on one case in which there has been positive and well-established indirect contact between the adoptive parents and birth parents. Recently, the adoptive mum said to me, 'I think we should exchange phone numbers'. So I met the birth parents and discussed boundaries, then I took their email addresses and the adoptive mother and her child emailed them. You have to think it through like a contact agreement.

A POST-ADOPTION WORKER

(See p. 29 in *Birth relatives* for more on contact with birth relatives.)

Supporting a young person

- Sometimes parents and teenagers just can't talk to each other without arguing. It can make things easier for everyone if the young person can talk to an experienced social worker, with the agreement of his parents, who can explain how to go about things for the best chance of a good outcome.

- Empathise with the young person that his life is much more complex than that of his friends.

- It is important to talk about the young person's reason for wanting to seek contact. It may be that, with more information about his past and family of origin, he will decide for himself that now is not the right time.

- Once you have talked, it may help if you then give the young person some time to think things through.

- Some young people become even more determined if they think people are opposed to something they want to do. But adoptive parents may understandably feel apprehensive or even fearful at the thought of their child meeting his birth parents.

- Adopted people have a right to know about their birth family. So the questions are "what is the best way?" and "when is the right time?", not whether the child should know or not. (Parents need to understand that this conversation is different from a discussion they might have with their child about drugs, for example.) Timing is a grey area, on which parents and teenagers may have differing views. Teenagers need to feel that adults respect their point of view.

- The better the relationship between the birth parents and adoptive parents, the more protective this is for the child. It may be a good idea if the adoptive parents could meet the birth parent(s) first, if the young person does want to meet his birth parent(s). An adoption support worker could be present to facilitate this.

- If contact is arranged, it may not be appropriate for the adoptive parents to be involved in every aspect of this - for instance, they could bring their child to the meeting but not be present when he actually meets his birth relative.

- Certainly in some cases birth relatives pose a risk and you would not wish to encourage or facilitate any contact between them and the young person. A risk assessment should be undertaken in these situations, which will inform whether and how contact should be arranged.

- However, if the young person were to simply initiate contact on his own, you would have no chance of supporting him or helping him manage the situation. So it is important to explain what you know and give reasons for your advice and decisions.

  Try to ensure that the child or young person has a good understanding of the complexities of making contact with birth relatives and where it can lead.

Helping young people understand the implications of contact via Facebook

Children are capable of using the internet to search for information at a young age and often it's their first point of reference when there is something they want to know or when they have a problem of any kind.

Obviously, the ideal is for an adopted child to ask his adoptive parents if he wants to know about his birth family, rather than searching in secret on the internet. But increasingly, young people who want up-to-date information about their birth parents are looking for it on Facebook. There is a risk that they could come across upsetting or disturbing material from or about their birth families, with no support. If they make contact, they can easily get themselves in too deep, too soon, and not be able to cope with this.

> *How many disaffected (goes with the territory!) young teens are going to be exposed to risk in this way? I think guides for young people are essential and training in how to keep themselves safe. I am saddened that the careful process put in place to protect and support adopted people with tracing or being traced (including their right for a veto) seems so significantly compromised.*
>
> LYNDA GILBERT, POLICY CONSULTANT TO ADOPTION UK

Encourage young people to think about the possible outcomes of making contact in different ways:

- Family relationships can be complicated. Is he assuming that his birth relatives will automatically welcome direct contact? Remind him that it would come as a shock to them. Birth parents may have all sorts of issues and problems in their own lives at this time that you don't know about (as well as the ones you do).

- To have their child turn up in their lives out of the blue could have serious repercussions for some birth parents (see p. 32).

- Going about it in the right way and making the initial approach through an intermediary (e.g. from the agency or local authority) gives the person time to think and absorb the news rather than reacting instantly – the outcome is more likely to be positive.

- Even though a young person may think he can handle it, there's no way of controlling the way things could develop – it could snowball in a way that he didn't expect.

Teenagers, however, have always demanded the right to make their own mistakes. Sometimes they will do risky or frankly dangerous things, no matter what you do or say.

(Part 3 looks at how to manage situations in which there is or has been direct contact between young adopted people and their birth relatives.)

Adoptive parents

Often, a young person's need to know about his birth parents peaks at the same time that the conflicts of adolescence are affecting his relationships with his adoptive parents. Sometimes adoptive parents feel hurt or threatened by their child's need to know about his birth parents and/or brothers and sisters. They may feel insecure in their relationship with the child, especially in the teenage years. Adoptive parents need help with managing their own feelings. They need support to increase their confidence so that they can better support their son or daughter.

The fact that my daughter's birth father searched for her meant the world to her – even though he is a schizophrenic who is in secure accommodation and she was told that it would be dangerous for her to have contact with him.

There is a powerful pull, particularly in teens, to either make contact or at least get some up-to-date information. Unattached teens seem to need to make sense of who and why they are as they are, and are usually not getting on well with – or sadly are even estranged from – their adoptive families by that time.

Teenagers (adopted or birth children) who have formed an attachment to their parents "know" they hate their parents, know they will NEVER be like their parents and generally find their parents a pain in the bum… they are secure in all of that. No matter how horrible the teen years may be, they can safely kick against their family, knowing and feeling secure that all will be well and they "belong". If only unattached teens could be helped to articulate all their angst and feelings…how different the outcomes could be for them. They make so many mistakes at this time in their life, during a period when they just don't feel like they "belong" anywhere.

AN ADOPTIVE MOTHER

Adoptive parents don't always know if their child has questions about his past or is curious about his birth family. He may keep his questions to himself, either because that's the way he operates or because he thinks they don't want to talk about it or will be angry or hurt. His adoption and birth family can easily become subjects that are never talked about.

A lot of adoptive parents are inhibited when it comes to talking about the child's past. They tend to say 'my child knows they can ask me anything they want and I'll tell them'. But that may not happen – the child may never ask. Parents understandably push it to the back of their minds. We say to parents that, in our experience, every adopted child does think about it.

AN ADOPTION SOCIAL WORKER

Encourage adoptive parents to share the letters they receive from their child's birth family through letterbox contact, unless there is a good reason not to.

Some birth parents will sign their letter "Mummy" or say "I love you very much and I miss you". Some adoptive parents can cope with this. But others won't let the child see these letters.

AN ADOPTION SOCIAL WORKER

Where such issues arise with letterbox contact, the adoption agency should go back to the birth parent and help them to be aware of the impact of what they write in their letters and look at how they can write something which meets both their needs and those of the adoptive parents and their children to enable the exchange to continue.

Telling the truth, even if it hurts

Some children's stories are particularly painful or distressing. Both social workers and adoptive parents have an understandable wish to protect these children from the truth, especially while they are young. And prospective adopters learn during their preparation course that "demonising" the birth parents could harm the child's self-esteem, given that he is genetically related to them.

So adoptive parents – and sometimes adoption workers too – skate over the harsh reality, from the best of motives. The child hears messages like: 'Your parents really loved you, but they couldn't look after you.'

But, particularly now, there is a risk that the child may one day find out the facts for himself by researching or making contact with birth relatives. Or he may, of course, hear a birth relative's version, which may not be accurate or truthful.

Confronting the reality of their birth family and the circumstances of their adoption is not something that any child should go through without support. It's far better that he hears the facts from his parents and understands what his birth parents were like and how they treated him. That way he is less likely to idealise them and will form a more realistic view of what he can expect from them. So if you work with adoptive parents, help them to understand the need for honesty from an early age.

You are bringing your child up in a loving, safe environment. If he was adopted while very young, a loving, safe environment is all he will be able to remember. When you tell a child 'your parents could not keep you safe', does he really know what that means or what his early life was really like? He may have no real understanding of what you mean. You need to tell them more and more as they get older and by the time they are teenagers they need to understand everything.

AN ADOPTION SOCIAL WORKER

Re-opening contact

If an adopted young person wants to find out more about birth parents and even ask for contact, through the adoption agency or local authority adoption support services, this can be initiated at any time – not only when the young person reaches 18 (if in England, Wales or Northern Ireland) or 16 (if in Scotland). If it happens before the young person is confident enough to do this independently, he may be more willing to accept his parents' help.

Children and young people can approach adoption support services themselves if they don't want their parents to be involved. If this happens before the child is 18 – or 16 – social workers must involve the adoptive parents and work alongside them while preparing the child and supporting all parties through any reunion. If it happens after the age of 18 – or 16 – it is up to the adopted person himself to involve his adoptive parents as much or as little as he wants.

If a child or young person has expressed an interest in finding out more about his birth parents or perhaps even meeting them, what should you advise adoptive parents to do?

- Firstly, talk with him and, together, work out what he does want. He may not even be sure of this himself. Sometimes children express a desire to meet their birth mother when what they actually mean is: 'I want to know more about my birth mother'. They cannot imagine how this will actually happen – give them some scenarios for where, when and how the contact could start and develop.

- This may be the right time to show the child his "later life letter", if he hasn't already read it and/or to do some updating work on life story work.

You can also encourage adoptive parents to seek support from local adoption support services such as adopter support groups or their approving adoption agency.

You could offer to do the following:

- Look again at the adoption files to find out more information about the birth parents so that they can share this with their child.

- Find out if there has been continued contact between the agency and the birth parents.

- Write to the birth parents for up-to-date information.

- Look into the possibility of setting up some letterbox contact now, if appropriate.

- Extend letterbox contact, if the parents have kept this up.
- Arrange for a meeting between their child and a birth relative – if it's appropriate, if both parties want it, and after a period of considering and preparing for this.

(See *Finding out about the birth relatives*, p. 31.)

Being prepared

Parents and adopted young people need to be prepared for a possible approach from birth relatives via Facebook or some other way. Adoptive parents should talk to their child and ask, for instance, what he would do if:

- He wanted to know more about any birth relatives?
- He wanted to contact birth relatives?
- A birth sibling or half-sibling contacted him on Facebook or other social networking sites?
- His birth mother or birth father contacted him on Facebook?
- Someone came up to him in the street and named his birth mother or father and asked if he was their son?

Parents are sometimes afraid that talking to their teenager about finding birth relatives on Facebook could perhaps put the idea into his head. This is possible, of course. But they need to understand that there are risks, too, in trying to pretend it could never happen. When and how to address this issue is a tough decision that every adoptive parent now has to make.

Going through the adoption agency or going it alone?

Many adoptive parents know their child's birth parents' names. And it's hardly surprising that some look for the birth relatives on Facebook. They feel that this is a useful source of information for them and their child. In fact, they can often find out a lot more about the birth family this way than they can from the adoption agency. But obviously, there are good reasons for making any approach to a birth parent through the agency rather than directly.

Adopted teenagers may not see it that way. They may be excited and impatient and incapable of containing their urge to get in contact, especially if they have already traced their birth relative through Facebook. Going through the "proper channels" means having to wait, and this can be a lot to ask.

Some families may feel they don't want any more involvement with the adoption agency. Or they simply prefer to go it alone and feel confident enough to do this.

Some adoptive parents manage contact with their child's birth relatives directly, without the involvement of the agency, and have found that email and other online contact can be positive and beneficial for the child. In fact, some young people find this "virtual contact" less emotionally demanding and easier to manage than "real-life" contact. And where birth relatives live a long way away or even in a different country, arranging a face-to-face meeting may be very difficult.

CONTACT REGISTERS

Adoption contact registers

Adopted people and birth relatives can register on an adoption contact register, a service which enables adopted people and birth relatives who want to contact one another to register that fact, and be put in touch if both have registered. The arrangements vary from country to country within the UK depending on where the adoption took place. Contact details for the country-specific adoption contact registers can be found at the end of this book. The adoption charity AAA NORCAP also has a separate adoption contact register for adopted people and birth relatives – details are also at the end of this book or on www. adoptionsearchreunion.org.uk.

Vetoes

If a person was adopted before 30 December 2005, then there is a facility for them to register a qualified or an absolute veto (in regard to being contacted) with the appropriate adoption agency (the agency that arranged the adoption). However, the facility to register a veto only applies to people who were adopted in England and Wales.

Making contact and intermediary services

Adopted people in England and Wales can obtain a copy of their original birth certificate when they are aged 18 years. The original birth certificate contains identifying information which can help adopted people begin a search for birth family members. However, the arrangements for obtaining a copy of the original birth certificate and also requesting access to adoption records held by the adoption agency are different depending whether or not you were adopted before or after 30 December 2005. This is referred to as pre- and post-commencement adoptions, following the implementation of the Adoption and Children Act 2002.

Adopted people in Northern Ireland can also obtain a copy of their original birth certificate at the age of 18. In Scotland, adopted people have the same right when they reach 16.

BAAF operates www.adoptionsearchreunion.org.uk, a website which provides information on locating adoption records, along with a searchable database of adoption support and intermediary services.

Requests for reunion: how it's meant to be

Birth relatives

Regulations governing adoptions that took place before 30 December 2005 in England and Wales set out that, once an adopted child is over 18, the birth relatives have the right to request an intermediary service with a view to making indirect contact. There are different legislative frameworks for providing intermediary services for birth relatives, depending on whether the adoption order was made pre- or post-commencement.

Birth relatives in Northern Ireland and Scotland can either contact the agency that arranged the adoption to find out if they are able to offer an intermediary service, or seek advice from relevant services (see *Find out more*).

The agency they approach to provide an intermediary service has to assess the application and decide whether or not it should go ahead. If the agency is not the same agency that was involved in the adoption, it has to contact the adoption agency to seek its views about whether it should provide an intermediary service. Birth relatives are not automatically entitled to have an intermediary service approach the adopted person on their behalf. In some circumstances, the intermediary agency may decide it is not appropriate to offer the service.

The intermediary service, usually an adoption worker with expertise in this area, would contact the adopted adult and ask whether they would welcome contact. The choice is for the adopted adult to make. They can say whether or not they want to take things further. Going through an intermediary service provides support and safeguards both parties' privacy and contact details.

In both cases, things proceed slowly, step by step, with preparation and support for both parties from the intermediary before any face-to-face contact is arranged. At any stage, the adopted adult can say no to any further contact. The intermediary keeps the contact details secret, and acts as a "buffer" between the two parties.

Adopted people

Adopted people aged 18 or over (in England, Wales and Northern Ireland) can find out about their birth family if they want to. They can:

- apply for a copy of their original birth certificate;
- get help from an intermediary agency to find out about their background and, if they want to, ask the agency to approach their birth relatives on their behalf.

> *My adopted daughter went through conventional social service channels, with my support and intervention, to "find" her birth family information at the stroke of midnight on her 18th birthday! Guess she was looking for a rainbow's end....*
>
> AN ADOPTIVE MOTHER

Adopted adults are entitled to counselling and support and to use an intermediary service to make the initial approach.

In Scotland, adopted people also have the right at 16 to see the original court papers from the adoption and any freeing orders. Again, counselling is available, but there is no obligation to use it.

Birth relatives

Birth parents' attitudes to the adoption

Most birth parents accept that it is best for their children to remain settled with their adoptive families. Most don't want their children's lives to be disrupted, to have them dropping out of school or running away from home.

Even if they accept no responsibility for the circumstances that led to the adoption and have a burning conviction that they were the victims of injustice at the hands of the local authority, they may realise that it is better for the children to remain with their adoptive parents – at least until they are 16 or 18.

Some birth parents, over the years, manage to get their lives together. They mature and develop self-awareness, realising that they have made mistakes and regretting them. Others are still living chaotic lives. They may be focused on their own problems and difficulties rather than thinking about their child.

But a minority of birth parents live for the day when they can "get their children back". If they can find a way to trace them or get a message to them, they will. They expect their child will want to come back and live with them as soon as he is old enough.

Professor Gillian Schofield of the Centre for Research on the Child and Family, University of East Anglia, has researched the experiences of birth parents whose children have been removed from them by social services. Thirty-two parents were interviewed and at the time, most of the children were still in foster care; 18 per cent had been adopted. Some of her findings are also relevant to birth parents whose children have been adopted. She comments:

> Parents' sense of responsibility or blame for the children coming into care varied – as did their levels of anger and subsequent sense of whether it had been overall a good thing for the children. This led to some very different pathways across the dimensions of acceptance, responsibility, blame and anger. For example:
>
> ● Parents who **accepted their responsibility** and the child's **need for care** at the time and since, **appreciating** what foster care had done for the children and valuing social work support.

- *Parents who were **angry** with professionals at the time but now accept **some responsibility** for the problems and see the benefit of care.*

- *Parents who remembered **accepting** the need for care at the time, but now talk more critically of having needed more support and think the children should have come home after the crisis was over.*

- *Parents who **blamed** and in some cases were **angry with the child** for being difficult to be cared for and therefore needing to be in care.*

- *Parents who were **angry at the time**, **blamed** social workers, did **not accept** the child's need for care and have not changed since – often becoming more angry, using years of "evidence" to support their "case", and often being dismissive of foster carers and the role they played in their children's lives.*

Another difference that was apparent was...

Some parents were stuck rigidly in feelings they could not resolve or move on from, particularly feelings of anger or grief. Other parents showed a remarkable ability, given their difficult circumstances, to reflect on their own experiences and empathically on the experiences of their children.

SCHOFIELD, 2009

Requests from birth relatives through the agency

Birth family members' wishes about contact may change over time – for instance, they might not have wanted contact at the time of the adoption, but they may come to feel that they would like to have some contact. They should discuss this with the placing local authority or adoption agency. If they have a request for something not in the original contact agreement, e.g. to be able to send their child a birthday card, they should ask for this request to be passed on to the adoptive parents. The adoptive parents can decide whether or not to agree to it.

This is the "textbook version" of how birth relatives should go about things if they want more contact. Increasingly, however, they are turning to the internet instead.

Birth parents posting information on the internet

Birth parents' expressions of loss and grief can be heart-rending and disturbing for adoptive parents.

CASE STUDY

My husband and I adopted a little boy (M) last April and it was made official this past December. The contact agreed with our son's biological parents is one letter a year only. Out of curiosity, last year, my husband and I searched for our son's parents on Facebook and they were both on it. The birth mother's profile picture was in fact a close-up photograph of M sat on her knee. She had also written personal comments about M and how she regretted what had happened/will never forget him. We thought the issue was raw with her and she would eventually change her picture and stop the comments.

Now we have formally adopted M but she still has the same photograph of him as her profile picture and often mentions him (as does her mother on her site), making comments such as she will never forget him and will come for him when he is 18 and that she regrets this mistake enormously. Despite the very serious injuries she and/or her partner caused M, I have always felt empathy with this very young woman; abused herself, in and out of care and not having ever had a chance. We met them both once and they were very juvenile, I felt I was stealing M from her at the time and her Facebook page now haunts me and makes me feel the same way.

I can understand that she still feels raw about the adoption but he is no longer legally her son and we are uncomfortable with the photo on her site, her comments about him AND that she will be accessible as soon as M can type "Facebook". We feel we cannot force the issue for her to take off the photograph as this could make her go underground and underhand and perhaps do something in retaliation that could hurt M emotionally. It is a very tricky situation to know how to deal with.

An adoptive mother

Birth relatives and Facebook photos of children

A number of local authorities have had to deal with several cases in which birth parents have displayed photographs of their children on their Facebook profiles and this seems to be a growing problem. Sometimes these photographs were taken before the adoption; sometimes they have been supplied as part of letterbox contact.

Increasingly agencies have begun to take decisions about:

- no longer requesting letterbox photographs due to the risk that they may end up on Facebook; and

- asking birth parents to sign an agreement that letterbox photographs will not be posted anywhere on the internet.

However, it is important that such decisions are proportionate and based on proper risk assessments. (See Appendix 2, *An example of a risk assessment for the use of photographs in information exchange (letterbox) services.*)

Birth relatives' inappropriate use of the internet

- A mother, whose daughter was adopted as a baby, posted the child's name and a message for her on a site intended for posting tributes to children who have died and condolences to their bereaved parents. At any time, if the girl "Googled" her birth name, she would have found herself there, along with her birth parents' details.

- Some birth parents try to trace their children by posting messages for them on "missing people" websites such as www.missing-you.net and asking them to respond.

- There have been cases in which birth parents post the child's picture on a website or on their Facebook page, asking "Have you seen this child?" – the implication being that the child has been abducted.

- Some birth parents use the internet to campaign against what they perceive as the injustice of having their children removed by social workers.

- There are online petitions, for example, to "stop the systematic removal of children by UK social services" and "abolish all secrecy in the Family Law Courts". One birth mother set up an online petition for her child to be returned to her.

Social workers who take children into care sometimes find themselves the victims of online hate campaigns by the children's angry families.

> *A proliferation of blogs and pages on social networking sites have sprung up...social workers and managers are named and vilified, accusations are hurled at councils, and court injunctions banning the identification of the families and children are flouted...*
>
> *Some of the blogs are hosted in the US, where the Constitution's first amendment, guaranteeing the right to free speech, makes them all but untouchable...*
>
> *Myths about social services – that they get financial rewards for every adopted child or that they are involved in conspiracies to remove families' children – are perpetuated.*
>
> WILLIAMS, 2010

In a few cases, if a child searches for a birth parent or other relative, he could find upsetting or disturbing content on the relative's Facebook page, for example, photographs of their parent drunk, or pregnant, or with another child, or pictured in provocative poses, and sexually explicit or otherwise offensive comments.

When birth relatives make contact

Birth parents rarely have malicious intentions when they get in touch with an adopted child directly via internet search/social networking, even if they realise that they shouldn't be doing it. (Of course, the contact can still be dangerous for the child even if the intention is not malicious.)

- They may be anxious about the child and seeking reassurance that he is alive and well and that he is happy.

- They may not know how to go through the proper channels to request information.

- They may feel frustrated and starved of information if adoptive parents have not kept up letterbox contact as agreed.

- They may simply fail to consider the possible impact on their child, assuming that he will be delighted to hear from them.

Going through Facebook is easy, instant and doesn't involve having to talk to a social worker. Some birth parents may not have thought through how an approach like this could destabilise the child.

Even birth relatives who are allowed some indirect contact may try to find a way of having unmediated, direct contact.

> *A birth father wrote a letter to his child in which he said that he had opened a Facebook account. The adoptive parents did not pass on the letter. They wrote back to the father, pointing out that contact through social networking sites was not in the contact agreement and was not acceptable.*
>
> AN ADOPTION SOCIAL WORKER

This is a good example of how a situation can be managed. It is important that when such issues arise they are brought to the attention of the social worker. The social worker can discuss it with the birth parents and give advice about what is acceptable within the contact agreement and also the potential negative impact of their actions.

Paternity

Establishing paternity can be a difficult issue. In some cases, the man named by the birth mother may not in fact be the child's father.

The man who had been named as the birth father of an adopted girl was putting photographs on the internet and asking for contact. We said: 'Before we embark on this, we want a DNA test to be carried out.' The test showed that he was not the father. The birth mother can't say who is.

AN ADOPTION SOCIAL WORKER

We heard from a birth mother that one of her daughters (who had left her adoptive home) had re-connected with a man whom she had named as the girl's birth father, but who was not in fact the father. This man is very controlling. He says he will follow the girl if she moves away.

AN ADOPTION SOCIAL WORKER

What do birth parents need to know?

Birth parents' use of social networking sites to make direct contact is a serious and growing problem. Adoption practice certainly needs to change to reflect this. Adoption workers need to do more work with birth parents around the time of the adoption and, given the opportunity, later on as well. Workers need to help the birth parent to:

- understand the contact agreement, if there is one;
- appreciate that breaching the contact agreement is unacceptable;
- understand why they should wait for reunion until the child is 18, if in England, Wales or Northern Ireland, or 16 if in Scotland;
- know what they can do at that time if they want to make contact through an intermediary service;
- understand and prioritise their child's need for stability in the placement;
- understand how damaging it could be for their child to receive direct, unmediated contact through a social networking site.

I just can't bear it that birth parents don't get help or guidance to put their children first and at least try to give them the things they need, either resolution or forgiveness or just NO contact if that is what is best for the children.

AN ADOPTIVE PARENT

The consequences of making contact through Facebook are unpredictable and this is just as true for birth parents as it is for adopted young people themselves.

We are currently working with a birth mother who has made contact with her birth daughter through Facebook. Her daughter Zoe is 17 and has a history of attachment problems and very difficult behaviour. Zoe is currently living with her boyfriend, their baby daughter and his family. She has approached her adoptive family, wanting to come back and live with them. They have refused to take both her and the baby. Birth mum has turned her life around and now has two young children and works full-time. We felt that we needed to visit her to discuss the (general) possible negatives of contact. As a result, she has been able to give Zoe pre-warnings, along the lines of how small her home is, etc, so that Zoe will not think she could come to live with her. Social networking sites have implications for birth relatives too!

AN ADOPTION SOCIAL WORKER

When children and young people trace their birth relatives

When a young person traces their birth parents or other relatives and makes contact, this can come as a shock to the birth parents as well as the adoptive parents.

Birth parents may not have expected to hear from the child until he was at least 18. They may have been feeling a sense of loss and grief for years. They may have been thinking about their child ever since the adoption and wondering if they will ever see him again.

Many are happy to hear from their child and will eagerly and immediately start communicating with him. Some have reasons for not wishing to be contacted. Others, without wanting to reject their child, have the insight to realise that this kind of contact might not be in the child's best interests.

CASE STUDY

Sonia, a birth mother, contacted us because she had heard from her 12-year-old daughter. She had had a message from Rebecca, saying: 'Hi, I think I might be your first child.'

Sonia told us: 'I don't want to respond, I don't want to do anything!'

She had never met the adopters and had never wished to have letterbox contact, so there had been no contact.

We rang Rebecca's parents to tell them what had happened and they were horrified. However, they are a sensible couple and their response was measured. They talked to Rebecca about online risks. Rebecca was told that her birth mother didn't feel that it was right for her to be in contact with her while she was still so young.

We also gave Sonia a great deal of praise and reinforcement for contacting us.

An adoption social worker

Some adoptive parents may react with fury if they find out that the birth parent has replied to an approach from their child. But at present, few birth parents have ever had any advice or guidance on how they should respond to an approach from their child via a social networking site. It's entirely understandable that they would not wish to ignore or reject a request from their child. What birth mother would not want to respond to a message from her child who was adopted? They may also be afraid that, if the child asks his adoptive parents, they will refuse to let the contact continue.

Birth parents – particularly of teenagers – urgently need guidance on how to respond if their child contacts them. At the moment, there is no mechanism for providing this, years down the line. It should certainly be covered in support groups for birth parents, but of course many birth parents do not attend such groups and steer clear of everything to do with adoption services. It could be included in information sent out as part of letterbox contact.

As with almost everything else about adoption and Facebook, there are no right answers. Every situation is different. Here are some possible responses to suggest to birth parents, one or more of which may be appropriate depending on the circumstances.

- Suggest that the child tells his adoptive parents about the contact.
- Acknowledge the approach but explain that it has come as a shock.
- Say they have to get advice about what they are allowed to do.
- Say they are happy that they (birth parent) have heard from their child but that they cannot have contact until he is 18/would rather not have any contact at the moment.
- Suggest that they (the birth parent) could approach the agency to request that some contact, or more contact, can be agreed with the adoptive family.
- Suggest that the child asks his adoptive parents about arranging contact.

What messages is the birth parent giving the child?

Some abusive birth parents may use "trigger words" in letterbox letters or emails to the child, which recall the earlier abuse. No one but the child himself would understand the reference. This can re-traumatise a child. Adoptive parents and social workers need to be alert to this possibility.

(For more on birth parents' messages to a child, see the section on *Unmediated contact with birth relatives*, p. 68.)

An adoptive mother was monitoring online conversations that her adopted daughter was having with her birth mother. She said: 'I can see what's going backward and forward between them – the birth mother is telling my daughter: "They are all lying – I never did anything wrong".'

A POST-ADOPTION WORKER

An adopted boy had made contact with his birth mother on Facebook. She told him, over the phone, that his birth father had died. He put out a "status" message on Facebook saying 'My dad is dead'. His shocked friends saw it and told their parents, and everyone thought his adoptive father had died.

The birth mother had no right to give the child that information over the phone. It was a sign to us that she hadn't thought about his needs.

A POST-ADOPTION WORKER

Finding out about the birth relatives

Sometimes an adopted child or young person approaches the adoption agency or adoption support services, wanting to know more about their birth relatives, perhaps with a view to making contact. The birth parents may be known to the agency through letterbox contact, for example, or because there are continuing issues with other children. Social workers may know about the current situation of the birth family or any likely risks to the child or young person if he renewed contact.

Before arranging any contact between the adoptive family and the birth family, you may want to know - if it's possible to find out - how the birth parent(s) views the adoption now. Have they accepted it or are they angry that their child was taken away? Perhaps no one from the local authority or agency has had contact with the birth parents for some years. If no one knows anything about them, who is best placed to find out? In some cases, an approach from an intermediary agency might meet with a better response than an approach from the local authority department which removed the child.

(See *Key factors to be taken into account when considering contact*, p. 79.)

Siblings of an adopted child

Things can get very complicated when siblings are in unmediated contact with each other. Siblings may:

- be in another adoptive family (with or without contact with other birth relatives);

- be in the care of the local authority (with or without contact);
- be living independently (with or without contact); or
- have remained with the birth parents.

Children and young people are often concerned about their brothers and sisters and try to trace them through social networking sites. When a child is in contact with a sibling who is in contact with a birth parent, he will often end up in direct contact with the birth parent as well. Social workers should consider the following:

- Is there a possibility that the brother(s) or sister(s) of an adopted child or young person could trace him (or vice versa)?
- What is their parent's/carer's view about contact?
- Do the brother(s) and sister(s) understand the existing contact arrangements (if any) and are they happy with these?
- Do the siblings understand the implications of making direct contact via Facebook or another social networking site?
- Do the siblings know that there are other ways of establishing or re-establishing contact with a brother or sister adopted into another family? Someone needs to explain to them what to do if they want to make contact.

Some adoptive parents would be reluctant to allow contact with a sibling who has, for instance, substance misuse issues or has been in trouble with the police. They might also be extremely anxious that this contact could lead to direct contact with a birth parent.

Potential risks to birth parents

Some birth parents do not want contact.

> *I have worked with a birth mother who has gone on to have other children, who is concerned that her eldest adopted daughter might find her other children on Facebook and we have talked this through and she is taking whatever measures she can to monitor this.*
>
> A POST-ADOPTION WORKER

In some cases, unexpected contact could even put the birth parents themselves at risk. For example, imagine a situation in which a volatile young man has heard that he was beaten and injured, as a baby, by his birth father. Since his adoption at a young age, he has had attachment difficulties and behaviour problems as a result of his early experiences. Now, for the first time, he can track down the birth father with whom he has been so angry all his life.

Other situations in which unsolicited contact could put birth parents at risk include the following:

- A birth parent may be emotionally fragile or have mental health issues.

- A birth parent may be ill or experiencing a crisis in their life.

- The birth of their child and the adoption may have been a traumatic time in their life, for instance, if the child was conceived as the result of rape. An unexpected approach from the child will stir up painful memories and difficult emotions.

- Some birth mothers belong to a family or community where sex outside marriage is taboo. Such women may have kept the pregnancy and birth and subsequent adoption a secret from other people in the extended family or community for fear of being punished or ostracised. If the child turns up in her life years later, the consequences for the woman could be serious.

- If the birth parents are no longer together, they may not have told their new partners and/or subsequent children about the child who was adopted. A young person turning up and revealing the truth could have serious repercussions for the parent and their family.

2 The internet and protecting privacy

Young people and the internet

Few of us can now imagine life without the internet and everything it offers. Today's children and young people have grown up with the internet. Whether they are chatting online, organising their social lives, shopping, finding information, researching for school homework or study, downloading music, showcasing their own creativity or playing games, they get a lot out of it. We shouldn't deny any child the opportunity to use the internet responsibly and constructively. There are many positive aspects to children's and young people's use of the internet, including the possibility of online contact with birth relatives where this has been agreed and is beneficial.

Social networking online is here to stay and we need to protect children and teenagers from the possible negatives. Later sections of this book look at safety precautions and protecting privacy online. Do read it if you are not already familiar with these issues.

Young people may be extremely capable when it comes to using new technology, but lack the life experience and the judgement to know when someone or something is not to be trusted. They tend to be impulsive. Some are mixed-up, rebellious, drawn to sensation-seeking and risk-taking behaviour. Some are keen to meet new friends and possible sexual partners. It's the perfect recipe for getting into trouble on the internet. Parenting a young person who is tech-savvy yet emotionally ill-equipped to predict or deal with the consequences of what happens online can make for a white-knuckle ride for parents.

Emotional, social and behavioural difficulties and online behaviour

Adopted children and teenagers are likely to be more vulnerable than their peers online. This applies both to the general risks, which apply to any of us and our children, and to the more specific risks of searching for or communicating with birth relatives online.

Many adopted children have emotional, social or behavioural difficulties because of their early experiences of trauma, separation and loss. These could mean that, for instance:

- They may be suggestible and easily led (e.g. by a paedophile posing as a young person in an internet chatroom or by a manipulative birth relative).

- They may not recognise risk or may actively seek out risky situations.

- They may find it difficult to interact with others, to empathise and to know whom to trust.

- They may be naïve and easily deceived.

- They may be over-confident and believe they are invulnerable.

- They may be impatient and impulsive.

- If they tend to get into arguments and fights in the real world, this can escalate online and vice versa.

- If they are victims of bullying in the real world, they are likely to be vulnerable to cyberbullying too.

- Because of their early experiences, some young people may be drawn to seeking out disturbing or otherwise unsuitable content on the internet and engage in risky and sexually harmful behaviour online.

- They may express their anger, pain and frustration online in harmful or inappropriate ways.

- Those who have not developed a strong attachment to their adoptive parents are even less likely than other young people to seek their parents' advice or tell them when they are getting out of their depth.

- While searching online for birth relatives, e.g. people with a particular surname, they may make online contact with strangers who could use this as an opportunity to dupe and exploit them.

- Arranging secret meetings with people (including birth relatives) they have met online could involve travelling to an unfamiliar area, alone, and could put them at risk of physical as well as emotional harm.

> *Cyberspace is a haven for adopted people because they can reinvent themselves all over again. They may have a difficult time knowing who they are, having lived without any genetic validation for so many years, and they can now become whoever they want to become via the internet. They don't seem to understand that the people with whom they are chatting are also reinventing themselves. There is a lot of lying going on on the internet.*
>
> VERRIER, 2010

(For more information on internet safety for all age groups, see *Finding out more* at the end of this book.)

Social use of the internet: a beginner's guide

Social use of the internet refers to the way people use the internet to interact with other people: posting messages, swapping jokes and tips, asking for or giving information or support to others, finding new and old friends, having online conversations and relationships, sharing photographs, videos, music, opinions and much more.

> *Seventy-six per cent of young people say the internet means their friends are there whenever they need them.*
>
> THE FUTURES COMPANY/YOUTHNET SURVEY 2009

Many mobile phones are now internet-enabled – so in order to access the internet and use many of the applications below, often the only technology needed is a mobile phone.

If you don't know the first thing about the internet, here is a brief introduction.

Different applications

Search engines

Google is the most widely-used search engine. Simply typing someone's name into Google (www.google.com) or another search engine reveals links to any information about them on websites across the whole of the internet. In some cases, this will include certain information from social networking sites such as Facebook. The search engine may lead you to their Facebook profile but you may not be able to see all the personal information on their profile (there is more information about Facebook below).

Instant messaging

Instant messaging (IM) allows friends who have exchanged their email addresses to send messages to each other in real time, when they are online at the same time. This is done through instant-messaging services provided by internet service providers (e.g. AOL Instant Messenger, Windows Live Messenger). You can also instant-message via social networking sites such as Facebook and many other websites, such as gaming websites. You can also send and receive instant messages from most mobile phones (see *Mobile phones*, below).

Internet chatrooms

Chatrooms allow several users who are online at the same time to exchange instant messages with each other. People don't identify themselves – they use a "username" instead. Chatrooms can allow young people to share their interests and get emotional support from their peers.

However, the nature of this kind of communication can also disinhibit people and lead them to do and say things that they wouldn't do in "real life". Some chatrooms are geared to people who want to use them for sexual gratification. There is often name-calling and other unpleasant behaviour. There have also been a number of cases in which paedophiles have targeted young people in chatrooms by pretending to be another young person.

Games consoles

Games consoles such as Nintendo DS, Sony Playstation 3 and Nintendo Wii can be used to access the internet – a child may be playing computer games and be instant-messaging people at the same time. Parents should be aware of the need for parental controls for games consoles as well as computers.

Skype

This is an application which allows people to speak to each other over the internet free of charge. It means you can have a "proper" conversation without big phone bills. If users have a webcam (a camera incorporated in or attached to their computer), they can see each other as well. Skype can be a useful tool for adoptive parents who want their child to be able to keep in touch with birth brothers and sisters or other relatives elsewhere in the UK or even another country.

Bebo

Bebo is an acronym for Blog Early, Blog Often. It is a social networking site which was founded in January 2005. The company itself describes the site as providing 'an open, engaging and fun environment that empowers a new generation to discover, connect and express themselves'. Bebo is similar to other social networking sites, offering the user the chance to set up a profile, which includes a comments section for messages, and a list of the user's friends. Many more modules can be added, as can photos and videos; it also offer the opportunity to join various groups and link the Bebo profile to other services. Three privacy levels are offered: public, private and fully private. Public profiles can be seen by anyone except that profiles of users younger than 16 are seen only by logged-in users; private profiles can only be seen by friends and members of any group the user has joined; while fully private profiles are ones where the user has not joined any group, so only their direct friends can view the profile.

Tracing websites

The internet is home to a huge number of "where are you now?" and "missing people" sites as well as organisations (commercial and non-profit) that offer to help you trace people you've lost touch with or research your family tree.

In common with other websites, these sites often have discussion boards or message boards on which people can leave messages for others, including people they are searching for.

The Missing You website (www.missing-you.net) has literally thousands of messages posted by people who are searching for someone. There is an adoption section which lists messages from adult adopted people searching for birth relatives or from birth relatives looking for family members adopted many years earlier. In one or two of the messages, it is clear that birth mothers are addressing their young children who are living with adoptive families.

On the Genes Reunited site (www.genesreunited.co.uk), people can register in the hope of getting in touch with relatives – with obvious appeal for some adopted children wanting to find out about their origins, as well as birth relatives hoping to trace children.

Websites and groups for birth parents

There are a number of websites for "self-help" organisations for people whose children have gone through or are going through care proceedings, or whose children have been adopted.

There are Facebook groups for people interesting in tracing family members (e.g. Familylink) and groups started by parents who are aggrieved that their children have been removed by social services.

YouTube

This is a site on which people can post videos so that other people can access them via the internet. For instance, an aspiring band might put a video of themselves on YouTube. In some cases, people recommend a video clip to their friends, who recommend it to their friends and it ends up "going viral" and being seen by thousands or millions of people around the world.

YouTube can also be used in a sinister way – there have been many cases of assaults and bullying being recorded on mobile phones and posted on the internet for others to view.

Flickr

This is a photo-sharing website.

Blogs

Blogs are websites – weblogs – with regularly updated content. If you write a blog, you write regular instalments rather like a diary and post them on the internet for others to read.

Twitter

"Tweeting" is like blogging (above) but the messages are very short. People subscribe to another person's (or organisation's) Twitter feed, which means they receive Twitter messages ("tweets") whenever that person or organisation sends them out. Tweets can be sent and received via email and mobile phone.

Mobile phones

From my own experience of such tasks as supervising contact I have an appreciation of how mobile telephones have impacted upon a social worker's ability to "control" situations and relationships. They offer an easy way for two people, who should perhaps not be in constant communication with each other, to maintain that communication, and from the very narrow perspective of a social worker's need to sometimes preserve confidentiality and "manage" relationships, they now present a significant challenge.

AN ADOPTION SUPPORT WORKER

- Many mobile phones can also be used to access the internet. So if parents have set up filtering or monitoring on their home computer to prevent access to unsuitable websites, they may need to set up similar features on their child's phone too.

- Some people use their mobile phones to take photographs of themselves (or someone else) naked or in suggestive poses and then send the pictures, by phone, to someone else's phone ("sexting"). Sometimes girls are persuaded or bullied into doing this by boyfriends or men they have befriended online. Of course, these photographs can subsequently be used maliciously and circulated around any number of other people or posted on the internet where they may end up being seen by thousands.

> *Birth parents once tried to slip the child their mobile phone number during contact to ask him to keep in touch and have tried to give him a gift of a mobile so they could keep in touch with him.*
>
> AN ADOPTION SOCIAL WORKER

Location services on mobile phones

Location services, which can identify your location via your mobile phone, are becoming popular. A guide for parents from Vodafone explains the implications:

> *Until recently, the focus of location-based services was on personal location and navigation with the user asking the question 'Where am I?' Now, the focus is moving towards more social 'Where are you?' and 'Here I am!' services, where users opt into services within a mapping or social networking application.*
>
> HTTP://PARENTS.VODAFONE.COM/LOCATIONSERVICES

For instance, there are applications, such as Google Latitude, which let you share your location with your friends and family when you are out and about. A young person can sign up to use this kind of location service alongside her Facebook profile, so that everyone on her "friends" list can see where she is.

Location services can be abused. Think about the implications: if birth relatives are on the young person's "friends" list, they would know her location to within a few metres and might be able to work out where she lives or goes to school (as these will be her most regular locations).

There are also passive location (tracking) devices that use locations provided by the mobile network.

> *Explain (to your child) that they should never accept a mobile from anyone (known or unknown to them) without your agreement, as it might be pre-installed with passive location services.*

If you're really worried about location-based services, don't give your child a mobile with GPS or Wi-Fi on it or, if they already have a mobile, disable GPS or Wi-Fi on their handset.

HTTP://PARENTS.VODAFONE.COM/LOCATIONSERVICES

Children and young people and their parents all need to know about the risks and understand the precautions they should take.

For more information, read guides to mobile location services, such as those produced by Vodafone and Ofcom (see *Finding out more*).

Online communication: some of the risks

Because of the developments in social media, just a few of which are listed above, children and young people can potentially "meet" online not just birth relatives but a wide range of people from around the world with whom they would never normally come into contact.

In cyberspace there are well-documented risks which apply to all of us, such as:

- internet fraud;
- identity theft;
- hackers hacking into accounts to steal passwords and access bank details, etc;
- "phishing" – fraudulent emails that trick people into giving away personal details;
- online bullying, harassment or abuse or other unwanted approaches (either from known people or strangers);
- approaches from paedophiles grooming children for sexual purposes;
- coming across (or children searching for) content of a violent, pornographic or horrific nature;
- sites which could be harmful to vulnerable people, such as those which discuss self-harm or anorexia in inappropriate ways and suicide sites.

For more information: there's a huge amount of advice out there about how to avoid the risks (see *Finding out more*).

All children and young people need to understand *and put into practice* common-sense measures such as:

- never giving out personal details online;
- never meeting anyone in real life whom they have only met on the internet;
- knowing what to do about any online contact which makes them feel uncomfortable.

These measures, of course, should apply to communication with birth relatives just as much as strangers – but adopted children and young people may not recognise this.

Many of the usual precautions to keep children safe on the internet will, to a certain extent, protect them from being traced or contacted by birth relatives.

But adoptive families and adopted children and young people need to take extra precautions, which are covered later in this book (see p. 44 onwards).

Oversharing

Online communication is very different from face-to-face communication and people use it differently. People sometimes behave online in ways that they wouldn't in the real world. Some forms of communication, such as instant messaging with one other person, can feel very private and intimate. People may write things which they might not express face to face. They can be put off their guard and may be drawn into revealing information that they shouldn't.

Teenagers often share personal information about themselves and others with their friends, social networking contacts and even the wider web as a whole, in a way that many adults would find inappropriate or even shocking. They bare their thoughts and emotions, write about their experiences and relationships and post inappropriate photographs of themselves with little thought for how they might be laying themselves open. They may be less inhibited or may be rude or aggressive online in a way that they wouldn't be, face to face.

We have a 16-year-old girl on a Special Guardianship Order. She was given information about her 18-year-old sister and went straight on Facebook to find her. In our case this isn't a problem except that our daughter's behaviour on Facebook is now fed directly into her family who will be horrified to see how she behaves with her friends. She has an overpowering relationship with her boyfriend and there are countless aggressive arguments between them and friends on various pages. She has even had semi-nude photos of herself posted. The police have been to print off one conversation because the content led to the boyfriend's mother's car being damaged. She has all our relatives on her "friends" list and they can all see what happens and tell us they are concerned for her.

A SPECIAL GUARDIAN

Obsessive use of the internet

The internet is in your home – it's always there, it's always on. Many young people spend hours on the computer each night, chatting and catching up with what their friends are doing. Some parents feel that their teenagers' Facebook use is obsessive and they find it difficult or impossible to control it.

Checking for new emails and using Facebook can become compulsive, particularly if you are desperately waiting for a reply or you have a special reason to be interested in someone.

This young woman came across her half-sister and birth father on Facebook.

> *I have turned into an online stalker. That first accidental glimpse has turned into a low-level obsession. I check Lee-Anne's Facebook page every day. I have followed a link to a video blog that my father updates regularly with clips of himself doing karaoke and telling jokes. I now know where he lives, works and drinks, all information I never had before and all just from looking at web pages...I am fascinated by these people even though I know that what I'm doing is borderline odd. I don't want to meet a man who is only biologically my father, but I can't stop watching him either. I like the fact that I know more about him than he knows about me. I can satisfy my curiosity, without the fear that he will reject me. Nothing has actually changed in my life – and yet everything is different somehow.*

> *I HAVE NEVER MET MY BIRTH FATHER BUT NOW I AM FOLLOWING HIS EVERY MOVE ON FACEBOOK, AN ACCOUNT PUBLISHED IN THE GUARDIAN, 30.07.09.*

What can you do on Facebook?

Social networking sites such as **Facebook**, **Bebo** and **MySpace** allow users to link and interact with others online.

Facebook has by far the largest number of users. In 2006 it first became open to users in the UK and by 2010 it had attracted over 23 million UK users. At the time of writing this book, Facebook dwarfs all other social networking sites and it is the site that is involved in the vast majority of cases of adopted children tracing birth relatives. With Facebook, you can search for a person by name – you don't need to know their email address, which is the case with some other social networking sites.

On Facebook, you can do the following:

- Set up a "personal profile" – a "page" of your own on the internet, on which you can write about yourself and your likes and dislikes and display all of this to other people.

- Update it as often as you like, writing messages about what you've been doing or thinking about.

- Include links on your page to other websites that you like, e.g. charities you support or video clips or a blog.

- Link to your friends' profiles and, through them, see some of their friends' profiles.

- Send a request to other people (e.g. people you have met in the real world), asking to become their "friend" on the social networking site.

- Become a "friend" of your friends' friends, or indeed anyone on Facebook (if they accept your request).

- Post "albums" of your photographs on your page, which you can choose to make available for your friends and other people to see.

- "Instant message" your friends via the site if they are online at the same time as you.

- Read what your friends have posted on your "wall" – you and your friends can post comments, questions, jokes, and reminders for each other.

- Use the site as a one-stop social calendar to manage your social life, suggest get-togethers, invite your friends to parties and other events, and so on.

- Send online friends "gifts" (an icon or picture of something, like a birthday cake on their birthday) or a "poke" to say 'I'm thinking about you'.

- Join "groups" on Facebook to show that you like the same things, support the same causes or just agree with a particular statement (which may be serious or humorous).

Social networking sites such as Facebook are 'more important than family' to a quarter of children, according to a survey commissioned in 2010 by National Family Week. The study surveyed 1,000 children from eight to 15 across the UK. Twenty-eight per cent of children questioned cited websites such as Facebook, Twitter and MSN as the most important thing to them. For girls, the top three choices were popularity and having friends, followed by family and then social networking sites (chosen by four in 10 girls). Fewer boys chose social networking – their top three were family, money and then popularity and friends.

The appeal of Facebook and other social networking sites is clear. It's about your identity – who you are, what you are into – and friendship. Some young people accept "friends requests" from anyone and end up with literally hundreds of "friends". For some, the number of online "friends" they have feels like a measure of their popularity.

Part of the appeal is that a social networking site feels like an adult-free zone where they can express themselves however they want. However, some young people may misunderstand the nature of social networking.

> *Many users believe they are writing for a closed group of friends, unaware that the information they have posted may be publicly available and able to be searched for and read by a much wider audience.*
>
> CHILDNET REPORT

Online safety and protecting children's privacy

Adoptive parents need to understand how to protect their child online and how to keep their child's identity and location confidential. They may also want to know something about how to monitor and/or control what their child does online, e.g. which websites she visits.

Any advice you give to parents on these issues shouldn't be given in isolation. The best internet security in the world is no substitute for talking to the child about her life story, adoption and birth family. Parents must do their best to ensure that she is not struggling with unanswered questions.

Remind parents that:

- young people can be surprisingly skilled in finding ways of getting around filters and controls;

- if their child wants to be found by, or is actively looking for, birth parents, these measures won't stop her (though they will protect her from other online dangers);

- even if there are parental controls and tight security settings on the home computer, a child may still access the internet through friends' computers or computers at school or in a library or an internet café, or even her mobile phone;

- they shouldn't assume their child always tells them the whole truth...

There have even been a few cases of adopted young people who have set up a second Facebook account using both their birth first name and birth surname, with identifying details such as the date they were born, so that if birth parents ever search for them they will be able to find them straight away. There is no way of knowing how common this is, but it would suggest these young people have a strong and unmet need which is not being addressed.

Parental controls and monitoring tools

Parental controls can help keep children safe online. They can prevent children from seeing harmful and inappropriate content online and monitor their behaviour. But children and young people also need to know about how to keep themselves safe.

Using certain online security software (free or paid for), you can, for instance:

- filter out websites not suitable for children, by age range or category;

- stop children viewing specific inappropriate websites;

- set different ratings for web content for different members of the family, e.g. one for a nine-year-old and one for a 15-year-old;

- set time limits for how long children can spend online or block access at specific times of day;

- get email or text alerts when a child attempts to access a blocked website or when she posts any confidential information.

Fifty-three per cent of parents of eight- to 11-year-olds use parental control software.

OFCOM MEDIA LITERACY AUDIT 2009

There are monitoring tools which inform adults about a child's online activity without necessarily limiting access. Some of these tools simply record the addresses of websites that a child has visited. Others provide a warning message to a child if she visits an inappropriate site. Monitoring tools can be used with or without the knowledge of the child. Explaining all these and how they work is beyond the scope of this book. But there is plenty of information available online through internet service providers and other organisations. Or you can find knowledgeable sales assistants in computer shops.

Knowing more about what their child does online might alert parents to the fact that she is curious and is searching for information. It could be a wake-up call to let them know they might need to bring up the subject of her adoption and her birth parents. If she is able to talk about this, they may be able to help and support her with what she needs to know, as explained in earlier sections of this book.

Don't appear anti-internet!

The more adults know about the internet, the better. A child is less likely to listen to what adults say about the internet if they give the impression that they think it's all bad. She'll also resent it if they don't give her some credit for being sensible online.

A group of adopted young people were asked: "What do you want your adoptive parent to know about the internet and your use of it?" Here are some of their replies:

- *I am not stupid so you need to trust me.*
- *I know ways of keeping myself safe on the internet and I can show you.*
- *Don't knock it till you try it.*
- *It's not all about porn!*
- *If it wasn't the internet, you would only worry about something else.*

Checking which websites have been visited

Parents may wonder whether their child has been visiting sites such as Genes Reunited or Facebook. Searching the browser "history" will show a list of websites that have been visited.

Internet Explorer is the browser most often used in the UK. On Internet Explorer, they can click on the "Favourites" button on the toolbar (the one used to save favourite web pages). This will bring up three tabs: "Favourites", "Feeds" and "History". Click on "History" and the parent will be able to view a list of the web pages that have been visited. Parents can sort these either alphabetically or by date visited, or by most visited.

Remember:

- It's easy to delete the history, so if a child is attempting to cover her tracks by deleting it, the websites she has been looking at will not be displayed. She may have deleted the history because she's been looking at other "unsuitable" websites she doesn't want her parents to know about. But knowing that she is trying to hide something is a start!

- If a particular site isn't listed in the history, it is not 100 per cent certain that she hasn't visited it - she may be looking at it on a different computer (or via a different browser on the computer).

- There may be more than one browser installed on the computer, so parents who want to check would need to look at the history of each browser. It's possible for a young person to install an alternative browser on the computer (e.g. Mozilla Firefox, Safari) either intentionally or unintentionally (e.g. when they use certain applications such as i-Tunes).

It is also possible to activate a feature that saves the instant message history, archiving all the instant messages that have been sent. (NB: if a child has a separate account, in order to activate this on a child's account, the parent would need to know their password.) The way to do this will vary, but in Yahoo Messenger you do this: click Messenger menu; select *Preferences*; click *Archive*; select *Yes, save all my messages*; click *Apply*, then *OK* at the bottom of the window.

If parents don't want their child to see which sites on the internet they have visited, they should clear this data afterwards. (For instance, in Internet Explorer, go to "Safety" and click on "Delete browsing history".)

How far should parents go?

Internet safety organisations recommend that parents and other adults discuss and explain the use of monitoring tools with children so that they can learn appropriate behaviour on the internet.

If parents are concerned that their child may be at risk, they could decide to log or monitor her conversations, and this can be done through some forms of filtering software - but they should think carefully about the implications of this. If the child knows she is being monitored, she may feel that her parents don't trust her and she may start hiding more from them. If they don't tell her, how would she react if she found out? She might be extremely angry about it, and end up being more secretive and less willing to share things with them. Also, if they found out something this way, how would they deal with it? If she realises how they found out, she probably won't be in the right frame of mind to sit down and tell her parents what is on her mind. She might try to deflect the discussion by accusing them of "spying" on her.

Parents need to decide what is the best approach with their child, given her age and personality. Perhaps they could say that they are keeping an eye on things she does online and explain why. They can be matter-of-fact about it and say that it is their job as parents to keep her safe.

Parents have a responsibility to protect their children and they shouldn't be defensive about this. They should not be afraid of setting rules for their children's internet use or be apologetic about this.

Obviously, the child's age and track record are important here. With younger children it is often easier to identify acceptable boundaries. With teenagers, there are shades of grey as parents allow them more freedom and they become more resistant to what they see as attempts to "control" what they do.

Children and teenagers are entitled to a level of privacy. Is it ever right to read a teenager's diary, for instance? Perhaps you would if there is good reason to believe they are in some serious trouble or danger.

It has to be the parents' decision as to what action they feel is justified, given the circumstances and the level of risk they perceive for their child.

Can adoptive parents be their child's Facebook friend?

If adoptive parents are on Facebook themselves and their child will let them become her "friend", they will be able to keep an eye on her activities, who her friends are and so on.

It sometimes seems that adults and children are each trying to keep one step ahead of the other…

> *He doesn't realise that I can see what he's doing and thinks he can tell me he's not on his laptop but he is…I know he is because he's on Facebook and then he gets caught out and I tell him to go to bed through Facebook!*
>
> A GRANDMOTHER OF TWO, QUOTED IN UK COUNCIL FOR CHILD INTERNET SAFETY, 2009

Some parents manage to negotiate an agreement to be able to check their child's social networking activity (they should prepare to be surprised by some of the things their child and her friends share and the language they use…and be careful not to ruin things by writing embarrassing messages on her wall!).

But of course some young people would do anything rather than let their parents access their Facebook page.

Some parents resort to devious methods, such as:

- secretly tightening up their child's Facebook security settings (you can only do this if you know her password or if she leaves the computer while still logged in to her account);

- setting up a Facebook account under a false name so they can become her "friend" if she accepts the request (using a false name contravenes Facebook's rules, by the way). But see below: *Can adults contact children via Facebook?* They should think carefully about whether the risks justify this – it is a form of deception and could impact badly on their relationship with the child.

> *An adoptive mother who monitors her child's Facebook account sees that a birth sibling has sent a request to become the child's friend. She deletes it. It happens again. She continues to delete the requests but knows it is only a matter of time...*

As social workers and parents, we should always ask ourselves: what are we trying to protect the child from? Secret monitoring, banning and blocking are unlikely to be the best ways to offer this protection.

Things are changing all the time...

> *We don't yet know the full consequences for a generation that has grown up online, or the future implications of new types of search, for example, social searches, which aggregate information from across a range of social networking sites by your name or email address, or of the development of facial-recognition search software.*
>
> CHILDNET REPORT

Using privacy settings is vital

The following information will assist you in advising adoptive parents and young people. It is accurate at the time of writing, but remember that things can change, sometimes quickly (see also Appendix 1).

Using the Facebook privacy settings, you can limit the ability to view a profile and certain items on a Facebook page to certain categories of people, e.g.:

- friends;
- friends of friends;
- everyone;
- networks you belong to, e.g. those at a college or university;
- or you can customise it to include or exclude ("block") individual people.

Thirty-one per cent of 12- to 15-year-olds don't use privacy settings on their social networking profiles.

OFCOM MEDIA LITERACY AUDIT, 2009

In terms of how publicly available Facebook information is, the situation is changing all the time. Facebook has taken steps towards opening up parts of its site to internet search engines such as Google, a move which led to much confusion and protest.

At the time of writing, default privacy settings for certain categories of information are set to "Everyone". These changes mean that unless you actively change your privacy settings, certain personal information is viewable by "everyone" (everyone with a Facebook account) rather than just Facebook "friends".

Until their 18th birthday, young Facebook users don't have public search listings created for them, and the visibility of their information is limited to friends of friends, and networks, even if they have chosen to make it available to everyone. However, this doesn't apply to their name, profile picture, gender and network, which are visible to everyone.

You should leave the "city" and "gender" fields blank if you do not want them seen by people.

Certain information on Facebook is already available across the wider internet. And Microsoft has announced plans to incorporate Facebook messages that are flagged for the general public into its search engine results - so sooner or later, it's likely that Facebook will become much more "searchable" across the web.

- If you post something on your Facebook page, then - depending on your settings - not only your friends, but possibly also their friends or indeed everyone with a Facebook account may be able to see it. You can control exactly who sees each piece of information you post on your page - but many young people don't bother changing the default privacy settings.

- You don't have to be on it to be in it - even if you don't have a Facebook account yourself, friends or family can put photographs or videos of you (or mention you by name) on it.

- If someone is "tagged" in a photograph (which means their name is attached to it, as in a caption), "friends" of other people in the same photograph may be able to see the photograph. Facebook tells you if you have been tagged in a photograph.

- If a friend writes on your wall, other people may see what they write, unless you set your privacy settings high enough to prevent this.

- At the time of writing, you cannot stop "friends of friends" from asking to become your friend on Facebook (but you don't have to agree to the requests).

- Facebook also makes "friends suggestions" of its own. For instance, if A knows B, C and D, and B, C and D have a mutual friend E, it might suggest to A that they become friends with E.

- If people live and go to school or socialise in a small area and have many local "friends", it is highly likely that their "friends" will be friends with or even related to each other. So their names may pop up as "friends suggestions" for other people in the same village or area.

- "Friends" of course can sometimes change their minds about being friends. So instead of fun messages, young people can find themselves on the receiving end of abuse, bullying and worse.

Declining Facebook friend requests and removing friends

- If you want to decline a friend request or remove someone from your Facebook friend list, you can do this without attracting attention. You can decline a request by selecting "ignore". They won't be told that you have declined their request, but they will be able to send you another request in the future unless you "block" them. You will be asked: "Do you want to block this person?"

- If you take no action on the request they've sent you, they will not be able to send you another friend request. When they view you in "search" or elsewhere on Facebook, you will appear as a pending friend request until you either accept or ignore the request.

- You can remove people as friends by scrolling down to the bottom left side of their Facebook profiles and selecting the link "Remove from Friends". The person will not be notified, but they will be removed from your Friends list and you will be removed from theirs.

People are not always who they say they are...

As on the rest of the internet, people on Facebook may be posing as someone else. There have been cases of "identity theft" in which people have obtained other people's photographs and set up a fake Facebook profile purporting to be that other person, complete with photograph. They can then use this fake profile to "befriend" other people, either in order to gain access to information they wouldn't otherwise be able to get, or to target them maliciously.

Can adults contact children via Facebook?

It is Facebook policy that over-18s cannot use the site to search for under-18s. Facebook says that the default privacy settings on profiles of under-18s prevent them from being contacted by over-18s unless there is already a link between them (e.g. if they share certain friends or belong to the same network).

However, it is possible for this to happen in various ways, including:

- under-18s can enter a false date of birth;

- under-18s can change the default privacy settings to override them and make their profile viewable by adults;

- an adult can enter a false date of birth which makes out they are under 18;

- an adult can enlist the help of another under-18 to use their account to search for and contact the child.

NB: using a false date of birth contravenes Facebook's terms and conditions.

Controlling who sees you online

With most instant messaging services, you can choose which friends see you as online or offline by using "stealth settings". If you want to sign in but not let your friends know you're online, select the "Sign in as Invisible" option when you log in. Once you're signed in, you can see which of your friends are online but they can't see you. You can still send and receive messages, even if you appear offline. If you are already signed in and want to become invisible to your friends, change your status to "Invisible to Everyone". This will instantly make you appear offline to your friends.

With some versions of instant messaging services, you can appear online to some friends but offline to others. You can access individual stealth settings by right-clicking on a friend in your contact list. You can also appear invisible to an entire group (e.g. relatives).

This means:

- A parent may be online using the family computer while the child is using a laptop in another room. The parent might see that the child is offline and assumes she's doing her homework. But the child could in fact be on her laptop, using the stealth settings to appear offline (invisible) to her parents, while exchanging instant messages with someone...

"Blocking" people

If you receive an instant message from someone that you do not want to be in contact with, you can click the "Ignore/Add to Ignore List" button in the instant-messaging window to permanently block their messages. The person you're blocking will not know that you have chosen to ignore their messages.

If a child wants to avoid people who are trying to instant-message her (e.g. birth relatives) she can "block" them so they will not be able to send her messages.

You can also block individual people by name to prevent them finding you or contacting you on Facebook.

Searching for someone on Facebook

You can sometimes find someone by going to the Facebook site and searching for their name. However, if it is common, there may be lots of people listed with that name (Facebook has 400 million users worldwide).

Against some of the names there will be displayed a "profile shot", usually a photograph the person has uploaded to their page. Some people leave their profile shot blank or use an illustration, a general photo, a photo of their cat or their tattoo or whatever. You may recognise the person you are searching for by their photograph.

Even if there are a number of people with the same name and you do not know what the person looks like, you could conceivably send messages to all of them, to find out if they are the person you are looking for.

If you can identify the right person, you can go to their Facebook page. Depending on their privacy settings, you may be able to see very little information about them. But if their privacy settings are set so that "everyone" can see their page, you may be able to find out quite a lot about them. You can also see people's "friends", often with their photographs as well, and click through to their pages.

If you want to contact a person through Facebook, you can sign up to Facebook yourself and send a request to become that person's "friend" and, if you like, send them a message at the same time. If they accept your friend request, you can then see everything on their page that they have set to the level of "friends". For instance, you will probably be able to read messages on their "wall" between them and their friends, see their photo albums, find out a lot more about them and their interests and the places they go to, as well as being able to send more messages to them via Facebook. With this level of access it can be quite easy to find out which school or college a child or young person goes to, or even perhaps where they are meeting their friends that evening.

If you are in a person's "friends" list and you are both online at the same time, you can send an instant message to the person. Think of the implications of this: suppose a child has a Facebook page and has unwittingly accepted a birth brother or sister as a friend. She could be using her computer one evening and up pops an instant message from a birth brother or sister – they are online and waiting for an immediate response. This is why adopted children and young people should never accept "friend" requests from people they do not know personally.

There are various tools you can use to:

- hide certain items on Facebook from other people;

- create groups of friends (so you can choose to show the group and no one else);

- block certain people altogether (so that if they searched for your name it would not come up).

But remember that if adoptive parents block a birth parent by name, if the birth parent has already had contact with the child, he or she can easily re-establish it by:

- setting up another account in a different name and contacting her again;

- contacting her via the account of one of their friends (or another of their children);

- contacting her via the account of one of her friends (some birth parents have been known to "friend" not only their child but their child's Facebook friends).

Or, of course, a child who wants to continue contact could simply set up a secret second Facebook account in a slightly different name (or her birth name) and re-establish contact that way.

HOW YOUNG PEOPLE CAN PROTECT THEIR PRIVACY ON SOCIAL NETWORKING SITES

If you are advising or training young people about their internet use, here are some precautions you can suggest they use.

- They should use the highest privacy settings so that their information can be seen only by their known friends.

- They should not accept random unknown people as "friends". Doing this increases the risk of inadvertently accepting a birth parent or sibling as a friend.

- They shouldn't make public any information that could help someone identify them, such as their date of birth.

- If there is a risk that birth parents know their surname or if they have an unusual first name, they should use a nickname on Facebook instead of their real name.

- They could spell their name in a different way for their Facebook profile (e.g. N1ck Sm1th).

- They should remember that a person on Facebook may be using an assumed name and/or pretending to be someone else.

- They shouldn't use a profile photograph, if there's a risk that a birth parent or friends of the birth parents might come across it and recognise them. They could either not use a photo at all, use one in which they are not easily identified, or use a cartoon or illustration.

- They shouldn't publicly post any information about their school or local area (or photographs with any identifying details like car registration numbers or street names).

- To prevent birth relatives or siblings contacting them on Facebook, they could block them individually by name (though this doesn't stop a determined parent from opening an account in a different name or using a friend's account and attempting to make contact that way).

- They shouldn't display that they are members of groups or networks connected with their school or college as this could indicate where they live and even make it possible for someone to track them down in the real world.

- Even if a young person doesn't include any information about her school on her own profile, her friends probably do on theirs – and anyone viewing her profile can click through to her friends' profiles to find out about them and where they go to school. It may be safer for an adopted young person to hide her list of friends (go to the profile and click on the pencil icon in the top right-hand corner of the "Friends" box, then untick the box that says "Show my friends on my profile").

Remember that young people who want to be found may secretly sabotage efforts to keep their online identity private.

Facebook and adoptive families

- Some adoption support social workers use Facebook to trace the birth families of adopted people (of all ages) at their request, when other methods have failed.

- It can be a good way for adopted children and adoptive families to keep in touch when contact with birth siblings, parents and other relatives has been agreed – particularly if they are geographically far apart.

- Many adoptive parents have Facebook accounts of their own, either because they appreciate and enjoy everything Facebook offers; because they want to understand how it works; and/or so they can check what their child is up to and who her friends are.

Adoptive parents using Facebook

Many adoptive parents use Facebook to search for their child's birth relatives to find out about them or find out what their child might discover if she searched for them. Depending on their privacy settings, certain information may be viewable without necessarily becoming a "friend" of the birth parent.

If you send a "friend request" to someone and they accept, this means they can then see all the information that you have set to the level of "friends" on your own profile.

To get round this, some adoptive parents have used a pseudonym to set up a fake profile in order to send a "friend request" to their child's birth parent or other relatives. If accepted, this allows them to access information open to the birth parent's "friends", without compromising their own privacy in the process. Registering an account under a false name is against Facebook rules (although many people do use nicknames). Some adoptive parents feel this is also unethical, while others believe it is justified in the interests of their child.

If you become aware of adopters doing this, you should discuss the implications with them. Using deception to obtain such information could obviously jeopardise their relationship with their child or any positive contact with birth family members that might be sought in the future.

Some adoptive parents even print off photographs from birth parents' Facebook pages to show their children when they are older (one adoption social worker also reported doing this).

CASE STUDY

I actually have a positive Facebook story to report, in that I was able to finally see a photograph of my toddler daughter's birth father – and print it off for posterity in her life story book.

My little girl's birth father had refused to co-operate with any social workers by providing pictures or personal information – and the details supplied about him by the birth mother are very sketchy, to say the least. In fact, prior to tracking him

down on Facebook, I only knew, third-hand, one very random piece of information about him.

Mindful of having my online footsteps traced, I used an acquaintance's Facebook log-in to search for his extremely unusual - if not totally unique - name and came up trumps with the photo that I think will be so important to my daughter.

Parents sometimes wonder whether, if they look at the birth parent's Facebook profile, the birth parent will somehow be able to tell. You sometimes hear people say there are ways of finding out who has viewed their page. We asked Facebook: is it possible to tell who is viewing or has viewed your Facebook page (if they are not in your "friends" list). Is there an application that will allow you to find this out? Facebook said:

> *Facebook does not provide a way for you to see who's viewing your profile, nor can applications do this. Applications that claim to be able to do this violate Facebook's Developer Principles and Policies and are quickly disabled by our enforcement team when we find them or they're reported to us by our users.*

In some cases, adoptive parents have even received "friends" requests from their child's birth parents, who have managed to trace them on Facebook.

Friends and family

Where adoptive parents have concerns about possible social networking links with birth relatives, they should do the following:

- Ask friends and family not to "tag" their Facebook photographs with the child's name (or their own name, if they think this could lead people to their child); ask them never to use her name on websites, in blogs, etc.

- If they have been tagged in a photograph, use a button underneath the photograph which "de-tags" it.

- Get their child to tell her friends not to "tag" her in photographs.

- Prevent any photographs of the child appearing anywhere on the internet.

CASE STUDY

An adopted young person aged 14 found her birth family via Facebook. She had not disclosed her new name but she had given her mobile phone number. The adopters contacted the social worker who had been supporting them in relation to another of their adopted children. The adopters were extremely worried that the young person would be abducted. When they talked to the young person it was obvious that she felt contact with her birth family was out of control.

After discussion between the adopters and the young person, it was decided to close down this unregulated contact by changing her phone and closing her Facebook account. A new account was opened after a few months.

One of the concerns of the adopters was that, while their daughter's Facebook account was protected and did not reveal personal details, by accessing her friends' accounts personal information could be obtained by implication e.g. the school she attended.

An adoption social worker

It is possible to prevent your friends' accounts from appearing on your profile - untick the pencil box which appears above your friends' photos on your profile page. This way anyone accessing your profile will not be able to access your friends' accounts as well.

Facebook and friends suggestions

Facebook can suggest possible "friends" to you on the basis of your list of email addresses in another application. So, for instance, if an adoptive parent has ever emailed the foster carer of the adopted child, Facebook might suggest that the adoptive parent makes that person a "friend". If the foster carer had also added a member of the child's birth family as a "friend" (either knowingly or unknowingly) there could be a risk of the birth relative tracing the adoptive family through that link.

Does the young person have a Facebook account?

If parents aren't sure their child would tell them the truth, they can try going on Facebook and searching for their child's name (they should try both the adoptive family surname and the birth surname). If nothing comes up, she probably doesn't have an account. However, this is not 100 per cent certain. She might have an account that uses a nickname or a shortened version of her name. Or she might even have "blocked" her parents by name so that they can't see her profile!

- You have to be 13 to have a Facebook account but many younger children set up accounts simply by giving a false date of birth (though if Facebook is notified that this has happened, it will close the account in question).

- Setting up an account in a false name and date of birth contravenes Facebook's terms and conditions but is easy to do.

I really don't think there is any way of preventing this sort of thing, in all honesty. We have always been open with our daughter and talked about her past. She has never shown any interest in her birth family at all and never wanted to contribute to the contact letters we send to birth mum, which made this more of a shock. She was eight when taken into care, so knows only too well what her birth father was like. The birth parents are well aware that they are not supposed to have contact until she is 18 but that didn't stop them replying, exchanging emails and texts.

We are reasonably confident unofficial contact has stopped – but again, there is absolutely no way of knowing for definite. It is so easy for a 16-year-old to access email on friends' laptops, at school, etc, and to set up new email accounts.

AN ADOPTIVE MOTHER

Talking about Facebook with young people

If you work with adopted young people or are advising adoptive parents on how to talk to young people about Facebook, here are some suggestions.

- Sit down with the young person and talk about their Facebook page and who could view it. Some young people may never have considered changing the default settings or thought about the implications of having all their information publicly available.

- If she will let you, look together at her Facebook profile. Look at it while you are logged in (to another Facebook account) and when you are logged out, to see what is visible in both cases. You may be able to see who her other "friends" are and lots of personal information about her. Some young people include information that could enable someone to identify them, such as their date of birth, and locate them, such as their school, their town or village. (At the time of writing, Facebook, MySpace and YouTube all ensure that profiles of under-18s cannot be found through search engines. This should mean an adult cannot view details of under-18s or send them a message unless there is already a link between them, e.g. they have mutual friends or belong to the same network.)

- Explore with her how to limit who can find you in searches on Facebook and control whether your Information can be indexed by public search engines. To protect your privacy, click Account>Privacy settings>Profile information. Adjust your privacy settings for all 12 categories. Then click Back to Privacy>Contact information. Adjust your privacy settings for all nine categories. To control who can find your page by searching, go to Account>Privacy settings>Search. For Facebook search results, select "Friends only". Make sure the box for public search results isn't ticked (see Appendix 1).

- Ask her what she does if someone sends a message asking to become her "friend". Does she accept all requests, even from people she has never heard of? Or does she only accept people she knows and has met in the real world?

- Does she know she can vary the privacy of what she posts to her profile, item by item? She can restrict the visibility of what she posts to specific sub-groups of "friends". The default security options are set in the "Profile information privacy page" but you can choose new security options. You have to continue to make sure, item by item, that the things you post to your profile are only visible to the right people.

- Discuss why some people have to keep their Facebook profile more private than others – e.g. young people who want to apply for a job in a particular profession might not want potential employers to be able to check out their Facebook page and see what they get up to on nights out with their mates. And people who work in, say, the police force or mental health (or children's services!) might not want to be easily traced on Facebook.

- Explain that, in the same way, someone who has been adopted might not want to be easily traced. Talk about why being adopted means having to do some things differently from her friends.

- Without the right privacy settings, she could be contacted out of the blue by a birth relative through Facebook. Ask how she would feel about this. Perhaps she might want to avoid this because it's not the best way to make this contact?

- If she is receptive, you could suggest other ways she could keep her online identity private.

- Remind her that she can always ask if she wants to know more about her birth relatives or to make contact. Show her that you accept this is something she may want to do.

- The idea of keeping control in her hands may appeal to her. Explain that having the right privacy settings on Facebook and not accepting random people as "friends" means that she keeps control. It means she is the one who decides whether and when to have contact. This is better than having it thrust upon her when she might not be ready or it is a bad time, e.g. the night before an important exam.

- Talk about the nature of internet communication and how it's easy for people to do or say things instantly without thinking, which they might later regret. Remind her how, once you have given out certain information, you can never get it back.

- She may well be talking to her friends about her adoption and her interest in her birth family. They might even be urging her to trace them. Remind her that adoption is a very complex and difficult thing and that many people don't realise this. If she needs advice about adoption, you could arrange this from someone experienced in adoption contact and reunion, who understands how this can affect everyone involved.

All I can say is adopters need to be very careful about other people knowing the child's birth family name because even if the family don't do anything, friends at school may do something. We have found other teenagers encouraging him, not really understanding the complexity of it all, and so making him even more vulnerable. I think if some of them had known his birth name they might have done some digging too.

AN ADOPTIVE PARENT

Getting Facebook to take action

- Facebook is a multinational company based in the United States – where the US Constitution guarantees the right to "free speech".

- Its corporate culture tends to be about freedom of speech and freedom from regulation rather than privacy and safeguarding children.

- Within the company there is likely to be little understanding of adoption issues, and therefore Facebook staff may not understand or be prepared to respond to adoptive parents' concerns.

- Issues of unregulated contact or birth parents posting inappropriate material do not fit neatly into the usual categories of Facebook "offences", e.g. posting pornographic images or online grooming by paedophiles.

Facebook is resistant to getting involved in disputes about material which its users have posted online.

Complaining to social networking sites

We offer email support for Facebook because it enables us to most effectively and efficiently serve our over 400 million users worldwide. Through emails submitted using the contact forms in our Help centre, our User Operations team is able to verify the account owner via his or her email address and use automated methods to prioritise requests, making sure we're handling the most critical requests first. We also provide report links throughout the site.

A SPOKESWOMAN FROM FACEBOOK IN THE UK

Complaining to a social networking site can be a frustrating business. The European Commission looked at the policy and practice of 25 social networking sites across Europe that signed up to its Safer Social Networking Principles last year. It found that just nine out of 22 websites responded to complaints submitted by their users.

Many parents and social work professionals have found it impossible to complain to Facebook – though there have been some successes. Some families have had long battles with Facebook – one family ended up writing directly to Facebook's chief executive in California before finally achieving the result they wanted.

Some parents suggest writing direct to the head office of the offending site rather than using their reporting system and recommend sending as much information as you can and being prepared to persevere.

Children's services/social work departments also have difficulty getting social networking sites to take action. The Children's Charities Coalition on Internet Safety (CHIS) has lobbied on this issue. In its Digital Manifesto 2009, it says:

CHIS is concerned about the unresponsiveness of some social networking sites to complaints or issues raised by the public, and even a lack of flexibility in relation to quite delicate issues of child protection.

One example of this was an adoption case where the birth parent had posted a request for information about the child's whereabouts. The site where the request was posted insisted that the adoptive parents had to raise the matter with them directly, rather than through the adoption agency.

The site refused to respond to an intercession by the adoption agency that had placed the child. It should be possible for sites to respond to reports or requests from trusted third parties, for example, an adoption agency or a recognised child protection agency acting in good faith, rather than insisting that the adoptive parents identify themselves. That could compromise the child's anonymity and with it, the child's security. This example reflects poorly on the flexibility, responsiveness or even understanding of and interest in child protection issues of those running such sites.

DIGITAL MANIFESTO, CHIS

Reporting suspicious behaviour

In April 2010, Facebook agreed to set up new measures to allow users to report unwanted or suspicious behaviour directly to child protection organisations. Other sites, such as Bebo and MySpace, include a button which links directly to CEOP (Child Exploitation and Online Protection Centre). Users can press the button if they feel threatened or if they have been targeted by a paedophile.

Discussions are continuing and social workers and adoptive parents need to keep up with developments to ensure they can give the most up-to-date advice to young people.

Photographs and adoptive families

Uploading photographs and videos to the internet

People can share their photographs and videos with others over the internet in a number of ways, through websites such as YouTube and Flickr as well as on their Facebook or other social networking profile page and in photo "albums" on their page. Many mobile phones can now take photographs and videos too. All of this has implications for adoptive families.

Letterbox photographs

Increasingly, agencies have begun to decide to stop asking for photographs to be provided by the adoptive parents as part of letterbox contact in every case, because of the number of cases in which birth parents have put the photographs on their Facebook pages. There is also the risk that a photograph provided as part of letterbox contact could be a way of tracing a child. However, it is important that such decisions are proportionate and based on proper risk assessments. Some are asking birth parents to sign an agreement that they will not post any letterbox photographs of the child on the internet (though these agreements are not legally enforceable).

In most cases, sending photographs presents no problems and adoptive parents see it as something they are happy, or at least willing, to do for the birth parents. But some feel they are forced to do it and they would much prefer not to.

The care plan agreed for the child can sometimes result in adopters being advised to provide letterbox photos when they would rather not:

> *At present we are asking that social workers qualify why photos are to be included (in letterbox contact) rather than it being the norm. The problems we have are with the cases where the care plan included photos and this has been seen by the courts. In some of these cases, the adopters are asking to stop sending photos (in one case the birth mother is posting them on Facebook) but as it is in the court agreed care plan, they are being advised to continue.*
>
> AN ADOPTION SOCIAL WORKER

Social workers need to explain to adopters the benefits for the birth family and the child of photographs being part of a letterbox exchange and to take into account the adopters' views about contact when the contact plan is being drawn up and any risk assessments being made.

Where birth parents request photographs and adoptive parents don't want to provide them (or want to stop sending them), it is a good idea for the adoptive parents to write a letter explaining their reasons. This can be kept in the child's file.

Misuse of children's photographs

It is an unpleasant and distressing truth that children's photographs, taken by people who love them, can be misused by others. Some adoptive parents are understandably uneasy about the possibility of photographs of their children being used inappropriately.

According to the NSPCC's advice to sports organisations about photographing children, there has been a small number of cases in which photographs, e.g. those taken at sports events, have been digitally altered and have surfaced in child pornography on the internet. There are also reports that photographs of children are used as "trading cards" by sex offenders in prison.

> *If someone goes to prison and there is an agreement for letterbox contact with photographs, we will review the photograph part of it.*
>
> A POST-ADOPTION WORKER

Such cases highlight the importance of clear and well-informed risk assessments.

Birth relatives and Facebook photos

Not surprisingly, it can be a shock for adoptive parents to find a photo of their child on a birth parent's Facebook page. In some cases, birth parents even imply that their children are still with them, enjoying a happy family life.

- Some adoptive parents feel angry or upset or simply sorry for the birth parent. Some are outraged that a photograph of their child should appear on the profile page of the person who neglected or abused her.

- It could be considered an invasion of a child's privacy to have her photograph used in this way.

- The child (if she is old enough) could search for her birth parents online and come across the photograph of herself, which could be confusing or upsetting for her.

What should you do?

Adoptive parents who discover such photographs may ask for help from the agency in getting them removed from the birth parent's Facebook page. How should you handle this?

First, explain to the adoptive parents that it may not be done maliciously or to get at them. The birth relative simply may not have realised that there is anything wrong or inappropriate in what they are doing. Increasingly, people automatically post any and all of their photographs on Facebook.

You should be prepared to support the adoptive parents, if they are asking for your help. For instance, if there is letterbox contact with the birth relative who has posted a photograph or inappropriate message, the agency that handles letterbox contact can write to the birth relative and ask them to remove the photograph.

> *I would like to see the social worker in our case send a letter to say that, on checking on Facebook, she noticed the photograph of M and that the birth mother is no longer able to use M's photograph in this way and*

*perhaps even that further comments could result in the local authority
asking Facebook to shut down her account.*

AN ADOPTIVE MOTHER

If the photograph was supplied by the adoptive parents as part of letterbox contact, you
can point out that the photograph belongs to them. In this situation, many birth parents
will back down, realising that the adoptive parents could well refuse to provide any more
letterbox photographs if they don't agree to remove it.

However, some may not want to co-operate. Things can become even more difficult,
especially if the photograph belongs to the birth parent.

Can you get Facebook to take action?

*We were dealing with a birth family with a large number of children, all
of whom we have removed. They posted photographs of the children on
Facebook. We got in contact with Facebook and said we weren't happy,
but to us they were non-committal. Fortunately the family did eventually
take their stuff off Facebook. The legal advice we got was that these are
not looked-after children – we might be able to do more if they were.*

A SOCIAL WORKER

What can adoptive parents do if they object to birth relatives posting photographs?

*In certain cases, we may remove photos of young children when we
receive a report from a parent or legal guardian that the photos are not
authorised.*

A SPOKESWOMAN FOR FACEBOOK IN THE UK

If birth parents looking for their children post photos and messages trying to find the
child, can Facebook do anything to protect the identity of the child?

*It's a violation of our policies to post personal information about a private
individual in a public space without that person's consent. We remove
content that does this when it's reported to us by our users.*

A SPOKESWOMAN FOR FACEBOOK IN THE UK

The following general advice about photographs is given on Facebook:

What do I do if someone has posted an objectionable photo on Facebook?

You can anonymously report photos that violate our Terms of Use (e.g. pornography or copyrighted images) by clicking on the "Report This Photo" link below the picture. Facebook reviews these complaints and takes down photos as necessary.

What can I do if someone has posted a photo of me that I don't like?

Facebook will only remove photos that violate our Terms of Use (e.g. pornography or copyrighted images). However, there are some things you can do if you don't like a photo of you on the site:

1. To remove your name from a particular photo, simply view the photo and click the "Remove Tag" link next to your name. It will no longer be linked to your Profile.

2. Remember that you can only be tagged in photos by your friends. If you are having problems with someone constantly tagging you in embarrassing photos, just remove them as a friend from the Friends page.

3. If you don't want the photo to be shown at all, please talk to the person who posted it. They should be respectful enough to remove unwanted photos. Unfortunately, Facebook cannot make users remove photos that do not violate our Terms of Use.

Photographs: a way of tracing a child?

There is a risk that a child could be traced via a photograph – either a conventional photograph or an online photograph – if certain precautions are not taken.

If the child herself, her adoptive family or anyone else posts a photograph of her on the internet, there is a chance that the photo could be seen by a birth parent or relative who could recognise the child, if they live in the same area. Or someone might search for the child's name on the internet and then find an online photograph of the child which might serve to confirm her identity.

The chances of them identifying the child from the photograph are much greater if the child's name appears with it on a social networking website or if the child is "tagged" in a photograph. Without the right privacy settings in place, someone searching online for the child's name could be led to the photograph and other details that might reveal her location.

Suppose a birth parent has managed to find the child on Facebook (or the child has traced and been emailing her birth relative). If the child has a photograph of herself and the name of her town on her Facebook profile, this could make it possible for a determined parent to find her. If the child posts the name of her school, or the venue where she is going to meet friends one evening, the birth parent could wait outside and recognise her from her photograph when she comes out.

Facial recognition technology

The scope for "finding" people electronically is growing all the time: for example, a new Google service called Goggles uses images rather than words to search the web. At the time of writing, it is not yet available to use for faces – but this could only be a matter of time. Google is considering the privacy implications of this. But facial recognition technology is already here, albeit in its early stages. In future, parents will need to be even more careful with photographs of their children.

Precautions for adoptive families

Where there is felt to be some risk, adoptive families should be advised to take the following precautions.

- If posting any photos on social networking sites – for instance, to share with family or friends – privacy settings should be set to the highest possible level so that only people who are classed as "friends" can see them.

- They need to check the right settings are applied *every time* they post new photographs and not rely on the previous settings remaining in place.

- For a small number of children where significant risks have been identified, there may be a need to consider whether it is advisable to appear in school photos or feature on websites and in other publications like local newspapers and school magazines.

- If there is any possibility of social networking links with the birth family or anyone who knows them, no one should "tag" any Facebook photos with the child's name. Some parents ask their friends and family not to post any photos of their child at all and not to "tag" photos with any of the family members' names.

- If the birth parents ever met the adoptive parents, the adoptive parents may choose to avoid any risk of being recognised from photographs of themselves online.

- If the adopted child or teenager is posting photographs online, she should set her privacy settings so that only her known friends can see them. She should avoid including any photographs of herself in obvious locations such as in front of her house or school.

- Parents can refuse permission when schools and other organisations, e.g. sports clubs, ask for signed parental permission before taking and/or publishing photographs of children or filming them.

- Schools should take precautions not to put looked after and adopted children's security at risk – some schools do not allow any photos or filming at school events, except perhaps for allowing parents to take individual photos of their own child after the play.

- If felt to be necessary, adoptive parents should make sure the school and any sporting or other organisations the child belongs to know not to include the child's name on their website, e.g. in reports of sports fixtures, etc. They should put this in writing and remind the school every new school year.

- If there's a risk the birth parents know which area they live in and might be searching for the child, they may not want the child to appear in any class or whole-school photos.

- Photographs provided for letterbox contact should not have any identifying information on them, e.g. the child should not be wearing her school uniform.

- If adoptive parents are supplying a photograph taken by a photographer or had their photos printed at a supermarket, make sure there is no identifying information (such as their surname or the photographic studio's address) printed on the back of the photograph.

When parents are worried about providing photographs

Adoptive parents who have concerns about supplying letterbox photographs sometimes do the following:

- Supply photographs where it is difficult to make out the child's features – taken at a distance or in fancy dress or with their face partially obscured by a hat or food, for instance.

- Supply out-of-date photos from which the child is not so easily recognisable.

- Supply a picture that the child has drawn of herself, or a handprint or footprint in paint, instead of a photograph.

- Provide photographs in a format in which they can't easily be posted on the internet, e.g. in a keyring.

- Tell the birth parents that they are putting photographs and mementoes of the child for them in a "memory box" and that the child will be able to give this to them herself, when she is old enough, if she wants to.

- Agree to provide photographs on condition that the birth parent looks at them in the adoption agency's office and does not take them away (but remember it only takes a moment to take out a mobile phone and take a photograph of a photograph).

Some parents, who feel they cannot trust anyone to keep the photographs safe, refuse to provide any photos at all.

> *A seven-year-old girl lived with her aunt (the sister of her birth mother) and her birth mother was allowed indirect contact. On one occasion the girl's mother went round to the aunt's house when the child was not there, to drop off a present. A few days later, the child's photograph appeared on the birth mother's Facebook page. The aunt recognised the photograph as the one that sat on the mantelpiece in her home – the mother had used her mobile phone to take a photograph of it when she was left alone in the living room for a few minutes.*

Although adoptive parents' anxiety is understandable, it is worth discussing the wisdom of taking any extreme actions. In all cases, looking at the risks and balancing the advantages with the disadvantages will be a useful strategy to follow. Where possible, it would be helpful to get adoptive parents to learn to assess the risks so that their actions are well informed and not the result of anxiety, panic or fear.

CASE STUDY

Oxfordshire County Council had concerns about letterbox photos in the case of a three-year-old adopted girl. The local authority felt that, if the girl's birth parents had a photograph of her, they might use the internet and social networking sites to try to find her. It argued that allowing the couple to view a photograph, once a year, at the council's offices was enough to meet any obligation it might have under the Human Rights Act.

The birth parents challenged this and at an Oxford County Court hearing in 2009, a judge ordered the girl's adoptive parents to send an annual letterbox photograph of their daughter to her birth parents.

However, in May 2010 the local authority challenged the ruling at London's Civil Appeal Court and won. The Master of the Rolls, Lord Neuberger, said that the adoptive parents' concerns were genuine and that there was no justification for forcing them to do something they conscientiously and reasonably objected to.

The girl's birth parents will be allowed to view a photograph of her, annually, at the council's offices.

3 Direct contact

Unmediated contact with birth relatives

Facebook communication, often rapidly leading to the exchange of mobile phone numbers, is far from the ideal context for re-opening contact with birth relatives.

Making contact with unknown birth relatives - parents or siblings - in this way is clearly fraught with difficulties for an adopted child or young person.

- The things they are communicating are sensitive, distressing and raw. "Instant" messaging is the very opposite of what is needed.

- Emails and instant messages can be blunt and nasty, and contain accusations, recriminations, anger, grief, manipulation or shocking news.

- One or both parties may lack emotional intelligence and any awareness of how the communication could affect the other person.

- One or both parties could be seeking to make contact with a view to blaming, exploiting or abusing the other.

- Miscommunication is common - either party could be left feeling angry and hurt at what has been said, whether they have understood it correctly or not.

- One or both parties may lack literacy skills, which means messages are unclear or ambiguous.

- After online communication, they may be left feeling on a high and excited, or very distressed or angry, with no means of letting their feelings out safely.

- After sending an email or message, there can be an agonising wait during which the person is constantly checking for a reply.

- They may never receive a reply or the person may stop replying, and they are left feeling rejected and perhaps distressed or angry.

If the child or young person hasn't told anyone, he is alone and unsupported in all of this.

One father started sending messages to his daughter which started out pleasantly enough but soon turned intense and unpleasant, with comments like: 'If I can't see you, I'm going to kill myself'.

Understandably, some birth parents have been missing their children and longing for contact for years. Even if they have had letterbox contact, this is vetted and they may not have been able to tell the child everything they wanted to. If they do manage to make direct contact, they may to want to form an intense bond very quickly. This could be overwhelming for the child or young person.

In some cases, birth parents have behaved in the following damaging ways after making contact:

- bombarding the child with texts, emails and phone calls;

- passing on the child's details to other birth family members, which results in the child receiving this contact from several members of the birth family;

- undermining the adoption by trying to win the child's affections and turn him against his adoptive parents;

- rewriting history and denying any responsibility for what happened;

- demonising social workers removing their child;

- trying to persuade the child to meet them;

- dumping their own unhappiness, loneliness and stress onto the child;

- drawing the child into disputes they are having with their partner or other family members;

- drawing the child into their own damaging behaviour, e.g. drug or alcohol misuse.

Some birth parents whose children were removed because of abuse still represent a serious threat. Any contact – even email contact – could be extremely dangerous.

In some cases, the contact between an adopted child and birth relatives can be hostile with unpleasant or damaging messages and phone calls. Sadly, it can degenerate into abuse and name-calling – sometimes on both sides – with neither party seemingly able to detach themselves from the situation.

Here are some examples from adoption social workers.

A 14-year-old boy found his original birth certificate and traced his birth sister on Facebook. She didn't believe him at first. But her mother was there with her and joined in the Facebook conversation. The mother is in denial about the past – she is telling the boy that social services took him from her because she was feeling "a bit low" and that she didn't do anything wrong. He is now very angry and is saying he wants to go and live with his mother.

We have a teenage boy who is social networking with his very large group of siblings and other extended family. One of his siblings contacted him on Facebook and told him that he was about to have a new sibling. He was really worried as his birth mother has 14 children, most of them adopted with different families. The last two babies were removed at birth. Enquiries were made with the local authority where her Facebook page said she was living. They were able to reassure us that there was no pregnancy.

Some time later, our teenager remained really concerned that his mother may have moved and "slipped through the net" and have a baby that she is not taking care of, as he had now seen pictures of her on Facebook holding a baby alleged to be hers. (All my enquiries inform me the child is not hers.) So not only can young people find their family – they can now be taunted via such sites by birth family members.

Even when the birth parent is not doing any of these damaging things, simply having the birth parent come back into their life can have a destabilising effect on a vulnerable teenager.

As many adoptive families have found, contact can lead to emotionally devastating consequences. Often the initial approach is followed by a "honeymoon period" during which the child or teenager believes that finding the birth parent is the answer to all their problems.

CASE STUDY

I am the adoptive parent of a 17-year-old. We adopted our daughter ten years ago and she had had no contact with her birth father and no one was aware of his name. Four years into placement, the birth mother divulged the man's name, but nothing was known about him. Last March, just prior to her GCSEs, our daughter came into the kitchen rapturously excited because her father ("my Dad") had contacted her on Facebook.

It had taken him 11 minutes, from the outset, to get in touch with her – he had simply entered her two very distinctive first names, which we had not changed in line with current recommendations, identity needs, etc. He could have been anyone, he could have been a convicted paedophile, or, perhaps worse, an unconvicted one!

Anyway, it turned out he was OK, just inadequate and thoughtless, but his arrival on the scene threw my daughter's life off track, nearly ended my marriage and has caused my son to move out. She stopped doing any school work so got poor grades at GCSE, treated my husband like dirt, and he can't get over it, and idolised this other man and his entire extended family. I took her to meet her birth father and his present girlfriend and their new baby, our daughter's half brother, and she has spent a couple of weekends with them. Our daughter has got drunk, beaten me up quite badly, damaged our home and – among other things – spat at my husband.

I can accept the turmoil and identity crisis she is undergoing, but my husband and son cannot. The atmosphere between her and my husband (she had always been a daddy's girl) is very cool.

She is beginning to be more realistic about her birth father since the girlfriend has dumped him and doesn't want him around her baby. She has been able to accept that there is going to be another fatherless child due to his feckless behaviour and she has cooled towards him. However, she now spends nearly all her time on Facebook, like the friends who she used to say needed to "get a life".

She has put on weight, having been super-fit, and is drifting. She feels disloyal to her birth mother who has serious mental health issues, and with whom we have had twice-yearly letterbox contact. But she hasn't bothered to write to her, as she doesn't want to tell her about the emergence of her birth father and doesn't know what else to say.

Contact with siblings

In many cases, the initial contact comes from an older or younger brother or sister of the adopted child.

> I have had one case where adopted children have found each other on Facebook. Luckily these young people had good open relationships with their adoptive mothers and so involved them in what they were doing and it has worked out very positively. In another case, a young adult supported by our looked-after system found her adopted siblings on Facebook. Again, it was fortunate that the young people had good supportive open relationships with the carers and adoptive parents.
>
> AN ADOPTION SUPPORT WORKER

> Often young people who were adopted as older children are looking for their younger siblings. Just this morning we have had a phone call from our 16+ team about a boy in long-term foster care. He has been having contact with his sister, who is in an adoptive family, via Facebook and is talking about meeting up with her. This child is the youngest in a sibling group of five and we haven't heard anything from any of her birth relatives for several years. I don't think the adoptive parents know about this contact. I will notify them and let them know that they need to be discussing this with their daughter. She was only two when she was adopted – she won't remember why she was removed from her family.

Facebook has come along and caught us all on the back foot.

AN ADOPTION SUPPORT SERVICES ADVISER

CASE STUDY

My adopted daughter has a half-sister (by a different father), who was born soon after her and who was also adopted as a young baby. The half-sister's adoptive family moved right away from the area after the final adoption order. No letterbox contact was set up. They sent a Christmas card (addresses were allowed to be known) but nothing more. The parents were very security-conscious and were not keen on contact of any kind.

Out of the blue, five years ago, the half-sister rang our home and they spoke for the first time...no social services, just that. She was 13 and our daughter was 16. Then, of course, the girls started to have internet and mobile phone contact.

The two girls have had very different upbringings and it's an uneasy relationship. This half-sister doesn't seem to want to go down the conventional route to find out about her birth family and is trying to get my daughter to cough up all sorts of information. They go on Facebook a lot and she has been badgering my daughter.

I can't really trust what my daughter tells me, but she says she has NOT told this younger, unsupported person about the information she has about their birth mother...But personally, I would expect my daughter to get a lot of kudos and feelings of superiority out of dangling tit-bits in front of her half-sister. Their birth story is a horrible one to come to terms with and I am concerned that this girl is not telling her parents about the information and getting the support she will need. I am wondering if I should call up the adoptive mother and tell her.

Maybe this half-sister has traced the birth mother. With Facebook, it's so easy. I am sure as I can be that my own daughter would not contact her birth mother at the moment. She was very angry and disappointed about the things she found out when we went down the conventional route two years ago. It seems to me that with the internet and social networking, the already complicated adoption journey is tangling beyond ANYONE's control...and the fallout will be horrendous for many people.

An adoptive mother

In some cases, brothers or sisters still live with or are in contact with the birth parents. Contact with a sibling can rapidly lead to contact with a birth parent. Complex situations can arise, involving several families.

CASE STUDY

Sixteen-year-old Amy's adoptive placement had broken down when she was 14. She had letterbox contact with some birth relatives, including her brothers, but not with her mother. She started asking for contact with her birth mother when she left her adoptive family.

In spite of her history of abuse and neglect, Amy had an idealised view of her mother. But in fact her mother was a drug user who had been living a very rough lifestyle. She looked quite alarming – she was gaunt and unkempt, with few teeth.

Letters were exchanged between Amy and her birth mother. The post-adoption team began to assess and prepare both Amy and her birth mother in advance of any face-to-face meeting. But before the preparations were complete, Amy's birth mother sent her a message on Facebook and they began talking to each other.

Amy had moved from one foster placement to another and had ended up in residential care. Soon after the Facebook contact, Amy's birth mother travelled across the country to the residential home. Because she was 16, staff at the unit complied with Amy's wishes and she left and moved into the mother's flat.

Amy and her mother contacted one of Amy's brothers (who had been adopted), again by Facebook, and arranged to meet him. The brother met them in secret, without telling his adoptive parents. He was unsettled by the meeting and didn't want any further contact. When his adoptive parents found out, they were upset and are seeking recourse through the law in an attempt to control the situation. Their relationship with their son is strained as they feel they can't trust him. They also feel very upset and intimidated by the possibility of further Facebook contact from Amy, the mother and other siblings. It's not known if he is still in touch with Amy – if so, it is likely to be via Facebook.

Amy left her birth mother's flat after two months. The birth mother feels angry with Amy for not responding with gratitude to her offer of a home. But they have maintained contact. And she is supplying drugs to Amy.

Amy's adoptive parents have tried to maintain a link with Amy and be as supportive as they can but they have mixed emotions.

A delicate balancing act

Adoptive parents of teenagers and social workers working with young people have a difficult task: they must pitch their response at just the right level to provide protection without precipitating a rebellion which could put the young person at more risk. A social worker shares the following story.

CASE STUDY

A 15-year-old girl who was adopted when she was seven years old recently decided she wanted contact with her birth family again. Her adoptive mum supported her with this but wanted to go through the proper channels even though the girl did have a telephone number for her birth grandmother. The post-adoption worker arranged for supervised contact between the girl and her birth grandmother. There were two meetings, which both went well.

Then the girl's adoptive mother discovered her daughter and birth grandmother had been chatting on Facebook since their initial meeting. The adoptive mother felt she needed some control over this. She understandably felt betrayed by her daughter and was concerned about her safety (both online, as she was accepting friend requests from anybody with a surname within the birth family, and also in the "real world", if she decided to go and find some of these relatives who live in an area she is unfamiliar with and where she could be at risk).

The adoption worker had to handle the situation with care, particularly as the girl was making threats about running away to her grandmother.

Her mum stopped her going on Facebook for the foreseeable future (the account was in her birth name so she still had her "normal" account which she was allowed to go on with other friends) and the direct contact was ended for a couple of months.

Luckily the mum and daughter have done a lot of talking in the last few weeks. The daughter seems to grasp, to a certain extent, why her mum is so concerned – although the message she is getting from her grandmother is that her mum is being unreasonable as they have done nothing wrong.

The adoptive mum is ready for the contact between her daughter and birth grandmother to continue but there is a lot of negativity between these two adults in the young girl's life.

Mum has also told her that, during the time she hasn't been allowed on Facebook, she could contact her grandmother as much as she wanted by telephone/texting. She realised that stopping all contact could have the opposite effect and she didn't want to push her away.

This level of compromise seems to have worked and visits will start again next week – mum still hasn't decided when her daughter can go back on to Facebook as that involves contact with around 25 members of the birth family and she is unsure how to handle it.

Some of mum's concerns have proven valid. There have been a few occasions where the daughter has discovered something on Facebook from a relative and as mum has been oblivious to this contact she has not been able to support her daughter through some upsetting revelations.

So far, the mum and daughter have worked through the worst part by talking and agreeing to be more open. Mum felt she needed to get control back to protect her daughter but allowed some contact to prevent losing her altogether.

Some adopters flatly refuse to allow contact under any circumstances.

> *The danger of this is that they will drive their child to meet birth relatives in secret with no support. So much comes from the adopter's willingness to see it from the child's perspective, as curiosity.*

AN ADOPTION SUPPORT WORKER

Some want the contact to be put onto a more formal footing as soon as possible, so that there is more chance of keeping some control.

CASE STUDY

Jenny, an adoptive mother, found out through security measures on her computer that her 14-year-old daughter Courtney had been in contact with her birth mother. Courtney quickly admitted it and Jenny came to us for advice.

We asked Courtney and her birth mother, June, not to have any further contact until we could set up a meeting/discussion at which Jenny and June could come to some kind of agreement. We said that if either one of them contacted the other, we would like them to tell us. But a few days later, June did contact Courtney, who told Jenny about it. Jenny was very cross. Courtney was actually behaving more maturely than June. Courtney was asking for our help in dealing with it. Jenny was pushing for us to arrange direct contact because she felt that, without this, Courtney would go ahead anyway.

June was not a high risk person for Courtney to have contact with, but the logistics were difficult – she lived a three-and-a-half hour journey away and has three other children. We sent her a travel warrant to get her to meet up with us half-way, but she didn't turn up. I think she was avoiding the situation and was scared to face Jenny.

We are still trying hard to engage with her. What has helped us with Courtney is that we have known her since she was placed – she has had a trusting relationship with us.

An adoption social worker

The early days of contact

Some adoptive parents have made the shock discovery that their teenager has been emailing, texting and phoning birth parents or siblings and even meeting up, all in secret.

Sometimes, young people claim they searched simply because they were bored and mildly curious. Sometimes their friends urge them to search, or even start searching on their behalf, without realising the implications.

In some cases, things can move very quickly, from emailing and phoning to meeting up. It can spiral out of control, leaving the young person feeling pressurised and scared. Or the initial elation can be followed by a huge let-down.

> *A boy and girl adopted into the same family were contacted by an older birth brother, a young adult. Without telling their adoptive parents, they arranged to travel into London to meet their brother. But the brother didn't really seem interested in them and within half an hour of meeting up, the brother disappeared and didn't come back. They feel rejected all over again.*
>
> AN ADOPTION SUPPORT WORKER

Sometimes disillusionment sets in fairly soon when the young person gets to know the birth parents better. Birth relatives may lose interest and be unable to sustain the relationship. In some cases, the young person is shocked to realise that his relatives have difficulties of their own, that their lives are messy and chaotic, and that they cannot offer him very much.

The initial contact: what young people do and say

> *A young girl was contacted over the internet by someone asking if she was their daughter. Fortunately she told her adoptive parents and we discussed how to prepare her if this should happen again.*
>
> AN ADOPTION SOCIAL WORKER

Some children and young people do confide in their parents. It helps if the parents haven't made it a huge issue or told him not to have any contact with birth relatives. Sometimes, young people don't really expect to find anything when they enter a birth relative's name in a search, and then are stunned to find the person. Some feel quite scared and tell their parents at that point.

> *I dread to think what might have happened if she hadn't told us and had tried to manage meeting up on her own. She has not had to lie and live secrets, which would have been more difficult for her. I did feel invaded, which I wouldn't have had the approach been conventional, via an intermediary, giving us time to get used to the idea. I know our initial reaction to the news was not as it should have been, had we been consulted and the timing been more appropriate. It was all too much of a shock.*
>
> AN ADOPTIVE MOTHER

But adolescents are notoriously uncommunicative. The child or young person may be afraid his adoptive parents will be annoyed or hurt, stop the contact or ban him from using his mobile phone or the computer. Often parents don't find out until the child or young person has had quite a lot of contact, by phone and email as well. Sometimes there has been contact with several members of the extended family.

It can be difficult for some young people to find the words to tell their parents. They may be reluctant to admit that they are finding it too much to handle. Instead, they come up with their own ways of revealing what's been happening:

- One girl – accidentally or on purpose? – left a notebook with a "do not open – private" warning in a family room. In the book were details of her contacts with her birth family on Facebook.

- Another young person left his laptop open displaying an email he had had from his birth mother.

Sometimes parents can only tell there is something wrong because of their child's behaviour: his sleep and eating patterns may change, he may be isolated and spending unusually long hours online, often late into the night. He may quickly change the screen content when his parents enter the room.

> *A 15-year-old boy was having unsupervised communication with his older birth brother, without his adoptive parents' knowledge. His behaviour deteriorated and he became angry and began self-harming, refusing to eat and truanting from school. The communication was proving too demanding for him to cope with and was triggering memories and upsetting feelings from his past.*

Social workers who work with adopted young people may want to prepare them for what might happen.

> *Young people need help with the actual words to explain to their adoptive parents that they have made contact via Facebook or they are looking. They also need some form of words to reply if a birth parent traces them, to play for time so they can talk to their parents.*
>
> AN ADOPTION SOCIAL WORKER

Adoptive parents' reactions

Obviously, it is best if parents can try to respond in a calm, measured way rather than instinctively panicking or hitting the roof – but they are, after all, only human. They are likely to feel shocked, upset, lied to, angry, betrayed or afraid. They shouldn't make any knee-jerk decisions.

If they can manage it, they should ask him about it in a way which shows they understand that he wants to know about his birth family and that they are not blaming him for what has happened.

Adoptive parents have taken on the hugely demanding task of parenting someone else's child – and over the years they may have borne the brunt of the effects of early trauma on their child's development. Adopted children's early experiences can affect many aspects of their personality and their relationships. Over the years, adoptive parents do their best to help their child recover from his early adverse experiences and to achieve some stability. Once the birth family comes back into the child's life, they may feel that everything is under threat. It can re-awaken some issues they thought they had dealt with at the time of the adoption and put behind them. The thought of their child meeting his birth parents can evoke a welter of emotions: anger, fear, pain, sadness and great anxiety about his wellbeing and their own bond with him.

Often the child is thrilled at having found his birth parents and becomes completely wrapped up in the "new" relationship. He is constantly on the internet, emailing or instant-messaging his new-found relatives. All he can think about is his birth family. Adoptive parents can feel excluded, disregarded and hurt.

Sometimes, birth parents feed the child a distorted portrayal of past events and the child believes their version rather than what his adoptive parents have told him.

Sometimes young people start talking about moving in with their birth family, imagining that this will somehow make their lives better. A few do eventually leave home to live with their birth parents – although this often turns out not to be a sustained relationship. Adoptive parents have said this makes them feel that he was never really "their" child at all. They say they feel as though they were only looking after him until the birth parent came back.

What to do now?

Every situation is unique – with a different history and a unique combination of personalities, problems and opportunities. So there are no easy answers. There is no one right way to manage these troubling situations. Adoptive parents' own personalities and attitudes are also factors. Some adoptive parents will be prepared to consider supporting contact.

Although contact may not always have been in the child's best interests, this may have changed. Perhaps now is the time. If he initiated the contact himself, the message is that he has unmet needs.

Issues to be considered are the following.

- Did the child or young person or the birth parents initiate the contact?
- How much is known about the birth parents?
- How much information has the child given them already (e.g. has he told them his mobile phone number or address)?
- What is the likely motivation for the contact?

- What are the possible risks?

- What are the possible courses of action?

- What is likely to happen with each of these courses of action?

Some birth parents are dangerous and there would be great concerns about the risks they could pose to the child. But sometimes, if they do not pose a threat, the adoptive parents may decide that, if their child really wants to meet them, they would prefer him to do it with their knowledge and support rather than in secret.

> *Not all birth parents represent a threat and contact may well be something you could manage (for your child's sake) if you had to.*
>
> AN ADOPTION SOCIAL WORKER

Key factors to be taken into account when considering contact

If adoptive parents ask for your help when their child has made (or wants to make) contact with birth relatives, how will you respond? What factors should you consider?

When planning for a child who is to be placed for adoption, workers have to consider certain factors when exploring whether contact would be likely to promote the child's wellbeing. BAAF's Good Practice Guide *Contact in Permanent Placement* (BAAF, 1999) points out:

> *Equally it would be relevant to consider all these factors in relation to a child living in what is currently an "exclusive" (closed) placement in which the possibility of initiating or resuming contact is being explored, and when the benefits of existing contact are being reviewed.*

This Good Practice Guide dates from the pre-Facebook era. However, its suggestions about assessment still hold good if you are considering contact that has come about through social networking. The assessment, it says, should include the following:

> - *The child's wishes and feelings regarding contact; relationships with birth family members including siblings; emotional and developmental functioning; psychological resilience and ability to form or extend attachments.*
>
> - *The relationship of the birth relatives with their child; their views about the placement and about contact; their previous experience of contact; their health and emotional well-being and their current functioning.*

- *The views and experience of the current carers in relation to contact.*

- *A clear sense of the purpose of any proposed contact for the child, in particular, whose needs would it be meeting?*

- *The attitudes and understanding of the carer(s) regarding contact and how they could meet the child's assessed needs for any direct or indirect contact.*

- *Any conflict inherent in the proposed plan and how this is to be addressed.*

- *What administrative, practical, financial, emotional or other support (including mediation or supervision) may be needed, at least initially, to facilitate any planned contact.*

- *What arrangement is in place for reviewing the agreement and negotiating over time so that appropriate changes to the plan can be proposed and agreed by all parties, based on the child's changing needs and wishes and the circumstances of both families.*

BAAF, 1999

Managing the contact

Parents' first instinct may be to ban their child or teenager from using the internet. However, this is likely to antagonise him. If he is angry with them, it will make any dialogue very difficult.

Banning may be a short-term solution to allow a breathing space and time for discussion about what to do next. But it's not sustainable for long – there are, after all, many ways a teenager can access the internet apart from at home. He can use it at school or college, the library, an internet café, a friend's house, via his mobile phone and so on and so on. And then he will be doing it without his parents' knowledge and trying to manage the situation on his own, without his parents being able to offer any support or exercise even minimal control.

Every family's circumstances are different, of course, and everyone has to find their own way through. Parents may be able to accept that it has happened and try to manage it rather than trying to stop it. That way, at least, they have a chance of steering their child towards doing things sensibly, with the right support and safeguards in place.

To many parents, it seems unjust that a birth parent should make contact when they are not supposed to and then for everyone to simply agree that the contact should continue.

We have just discovered that our children's birth mother has made contact on Facebook. Both our children were under 18 at the time, one still is. In looking for help and advice via the original adoption agency, the local authority from where they came and our current local authority, it is clear that they all share these concerns and yet have no formal procedure for dealing with it. The incredible shock and incandescent rage is slowly subsiding as we have to now work out how to deal with it in the best interests of the boys.

AN ADOPTIVE MOTHER

There are, of course, good reasons why birth parents are supposed to wait until the child is old enough before requesting contact. If everyone just shrugs their shoulders and says: 'Well, the mother has made contact now so I suppose it might as well continue', what message does that send to the birth parent and to the child?

This is all true, of course, and it is important to acknowledge this. And sometimes parents and social workers can manage to gain the birth parent's and young person's agreement to stop the contact, at least temporarily, while everyone takes stock and agrees the way forward.

But birth parents and young people may not always toe the line, even if they appear to agree to it. If a young person wants to continue the contact and is determined to do so, he will usually be able to achieve this one way or another. Social workers and adoptive parents will have to take a pragmatic approach.

CASE STUDY

Sixteen-year-old Jason was adopted by Ben, a single parent. Jason is a vulnerable and damaged young man whose behaviour has been challenging – he has been in trouble with the police and has spent some time in secure accommodation.

Jason came home late one night and Ben asked where he had been. Jason said that he had been to Sheffield with his birth mother and other members of the family, after contacting them through Facebook. 'I'm going to move in with them. They are my real family,' he said.

Ben was wise enough not to turn this into a confrontation but he was worried about Jason's welfare and asked the social worker for help.

Jason's social worker, below, explains how she managed the situation.

Jason is becoming more independent and capable of doing what he wants. Ben needed to convince Jason that he didn't want to keep him away from his birth family. We advised him to make it clear that he wanted to offer support, for instance, by saying things like: 'Why don't I drive you over there so you can visit them for the evening? It's a bit soon to start staying over.'

We knew there would have to be a meeting to get everyone together but we didn't know whether people would be compliant. We arranged a meeting with a view to setting some boundaries and giving everyone space to air their feelings. I had a phone call with Jason's birth mother (Joanne) a day or so before the meeting – it was a relief that she came across as positive. Joanne said she didn't want Jason to be at the meeting and I had to relay this information to him – but in fact he turned up at the meeting anyway.

I also wanted to get Joanne's husband Nick on board. He was worried about possible disruption to their family, as he and Joanne have a nine-year-old daughter. He did try to keep out of the meeting but I wanted him to be involved.

At the meeting there was Jason, Ben, Joanne, Nick, myself and the locality social worker. I led the meeting and explained that this isn't how we would normally promote and encourage contact. I talked about how we would have preferred to do it; but, I said, this is where we are so we have to take things from here.

My aim was to get Ben and Joanne to work closely together to set boundaries for Jason and his behaviour. Fortunately they were positive to each other and together they could "lay down the law" to Jason. Joanne was able to stand back from Jason and work with Ben to tell Jason: 'This is when you can contact me, this is when you can stay over.'

We reiterated to Jason that you can't always do the things you want, because you have to consider other people.

Jason, Ben and Joanne all had their turn in talking about how they felt. That was important. It's not just about the practical adjustment – it's about the emotional adjustment too. Ben said that he felt a bit shunned by Jason. They had had a good relationship and he felt as though he'd lost his friend. A lot of the support I give will be to Ben.

Before the meeting, because Ben and Joanne hadn't met, Jason had been able to manipulate them. But since the meeting, the dynamics have changed.

This is always a delicate and sensitive area. If they hadn't all been reasonable people, it could all have ended very differently.

Research by Elsbeth Neil *et al* (forthcoming, 2010) on supporting complex contact arrangements has highlighted the importance of social work interventions 'that paid attention to the individual needs of all parties *and* aimed to promote collaboration and mutual understanding between adult parties'. For example, one independent agency said they would facilitate meetings between the adoptive parents and birth mother to build mutual understanding and collaboration, arguing that '...*adopted children can relax within contact arrangements if there is mutual respect...between the birth and adopted adults...they need to trust and understand one another.*'

Some suggestions for setting up contact

Adoptive parents and adoption professionals have done or suggested the following.

- An adoption support worker could meet with the child or young person and explain the physical and emotional risks of direct contact and why contact needs to happen in a safe and neutral environment.

- You may be able to tell the child about real-life examples of similar situations where direct contact (without an intermediary) has backfired and gone badly wrong.

- Tell the child you will help him, with his parents' agreement, to contact his birth parents (if it's safe to do so). If it's appropriate, you will arrange for him to meet them in a safe environment, e.g. in a supervised meeting in a contact centre.

- It is likely to be too distressing for the adoptive parent to be the one who liaises with and sets up contact with birth parents. The family may need support with this.

- You (or his parents) should talk to him again about his birth family history, explaining as openly and honestly as you can what happened and why he needed to be adopted, even if he has heard this before. (Sometimes writing it down in a letter is more powerful and he may find reading it easier than hearing it.)

- Challenge any misconceptions he may have about the past. Explain that birth parents sometimes block out the painful memories themselves. It is all too easy for people to rewrite history and portray themselves in a more favourable light.

- Remind him that once he has given information out to them (e.g. about where he lives), he can never take it back.

- If the child has birth brothers and sisters who have not yet been in contact with the birth parent, explain to him why they must not be drawn into the situation or have their right to privacy compromised.

- It may be possible to get adoption support services where the birth relative lives to engage with him or her. (In some cases, the adoption agency might have a better chance of forming a positive relationship than a social worker from the local authority which was involved in removing the child.)

- Whoever takes on this work needs to give the birth parent a clear message that the contact should not have happened; and that even if they are allowed some contact with an older child, there must be no contact with younger siblings.

- Adoption professionals should offer their empathy and support to the child and family – feelings can be volatile and emotions raw.

- Some young people are angry or under the influence of the birth parent and refuse to co-operate with any contact set up by the agency. Even if the child refuses, you may want to go ahead and set up a meeting anyway so that you are providing an opportunity for him to do it safely if he wants. That way, he cannot accuse anyone of keeping him from his birth parents.

You could also consider setting up a secure online communications service, or "virtual contact centre", as in the example provided in Appendix 3, titled *An example of a virtual contact centre that allows safe and secure email contact.* This particular scheme provides a safe way for separated parents to stay in contact with their children, and was designed primarily for child contact issues after separation due to domestic violence and allegations of abuse.

Direct unmediated contact with birth parents is difficult for an adopted child to manage (even if he started it.) It is a complex situation in which the child is trying to somehow reconcile his own needs and those of his birth parents; he might not be able to consider his adoptive parents at the same time. A child or young person in this situation is likely to need a great deal of support. Even when adoptive parents try their best to provide this, they may not be in a position to do so.

Professor Gillian Schofield's (2009) study on contact between long-term fostered children and their birth families makes this observation:

> *Children were left with the task of moving between the two "parents", managing the amount of information they passed about each to the other and somehow almost certainly managing the two sets of parents' anxiety about each other.*

And an adoptive mother has this to say:

> *My youngest admits to feeling very overwhelmed by the initial and subsequent communication with his birth mother. After a period of "time out" to decide how he wants things to progress, he has asked me to write (via appropriate channels) to ask that she does not make contact again and to leave the ball in his court should he want to do anything in the future.*
>
> AN ADOPTIVE MOTHER

The pain of adoption

Adoptive parents often feel their child's grief and loss deeply when he is first placed with them. They can empathise with the way it must feel for a young child to be taken from his family and placed with strangers. In most cases, of course, they soon "claim" the child and over the years they feel that he belongs in their family.

But, for an adopted person, being in a family that is different from his birth family is something that doesn't go away. Throughout his childhood and adolescence, he may live with a feeling of "not fitting in".

Nancy Verrier in *Coming Home to Self* (2010) writes about this.

> *No matter how nurturing, loving or affluent the adoptive parents may be, living with genetic strangers is a very hard life for a child; he has to spend*

tremendous amounts of energy trying to fit into a family in which he feels alien.

She discusses adopted children's experience of growing up in a family in which their own genetic traits (facial features, gestures, body language, temperament and so on) are not reflected back to them:

> *Those of us who have not had to experience this deficit have no idea what it is like to exist day after day with no mirroring of our genetic characteristics…It isn't until they experience the ease of being around their birth families that adopted people even begin to understand it themselves. Despite this difficulty, the main issue for adopted people is that of loss, the loss of the birth mother. If adoption is to be helpful to a child who needs parents, the adoptive parents as well as the professionals who work with them will have to first acknowledge the existence of the child's loss and the issues which ensue.*

Adoptive parents have to help their child work through the resulting pain. And the most important part of this is validating the child's experience.

But sometimes parents don't want to hear anything negative. Instead of validating his experience, the first instinct may be to discount what he is saying, concentrate on their own feelings ('But I love you just as much!') or try to offer reassurance. If, instead, they can listen to him and empathise with him about the difficulty of being adopted, then he will feel understood and will be more likely to share his feelings with them.

He will express how he feels only if he knows his parents are ready to hear it and strong enough to take it.

Genetic attraction

Social workers are already familiar with the issues around genetic sexual attraction through intermediary work but need to be aware of it in relation to direct contact arising through Facebook contact.

People reunited with birth family members often feel extreme emotions – it is natural and common for people to feel thrilled and excited and develop very strong feelings for their birth relatives. This attraction is known as "genetic attraction".

Sometimes the desire for intimacy with the new-found birth relative, combined with the attraction that results from the genetic similarity, feels like sexual desire. This is known as "genetic sexual attraction". In some cases people act on their mutual attraction and the relationship becomes sexual. Sex can be used as a way to become very close, very quickly, to another person.

The Finnish social anthropologist Edward Westermarck at the turn of the 19th century put forward the view that children growing up in close proximity are not sexually attracted to each other as adults. This has become known as the Westermarck effect. In adoption, when children are separated at a very early age, the Westermarck effect can be nullified.

Genetic sexual attraction is a "by-product" of a system which separates birth relatives from each other, particularly mothers and babies and birth siblings, at an early age. Obviously there is a strong taboo against sexual relationships between family members. Contact and reunion are difficult and complex enough for everyone to deal with even without sexual attraction becoming part of the equation. Social workers who are involved with adoption reunion may need to prepare people, in advance, for the possibility of genetic sexual attraction.

Contact through Facebook is often marked by very intense contact early on, in contrast to the conventional, mediated route to reunion which allows people time to get to know each other over a longer period.

It may not be always possible to prevent genetic sexual attraction from happening. Those affected feel that they are in the grip of very powerful and overwhelming feelings. But if people know about it, at least they will have some understanding of why this is happening to them.

It's important to arrange for specialist counselling, for instance, from a specialist service with expertise in this very sensitive area.

ADOPTION SUPPORT SERVICES

The need for adoption support does not end after placement when a child becomes settled with his adoptive family. As we have seen, new challenges can arise at different stages during childhood and the teenage years. The Adoption and Children Act 2002 (England and Wales) and the Adoption and Children (Scotland) Act 2007 recognised that adopted children and their families may need support at any time in the years after the adoption.

Local authorities (Health and Social Care Trusts in Northern Ireland) are responsible for providing a comprehensive adoption support service in their area. Under the Adoption Support Services Regulations 2005 (England and Wales) and the Adoption Support Services and Allowances (Scotland) Regulations 2009, local authorities must provide a range of support services in their area to people affected by adoption.

Support services that might be relevant in situations involving unmediated contact through social networking could include:

- assistance, including mediation services, in relation to contact between the adopted child and others, including birth parents and birth brothers and sisters;

- help for adoptive parents to ensure the adoptive relationship continues, including respite care and training to meet any special needs the child has;

- help where there is the risk of an adoption arrangement disrupting or when it has actually disrupted;

- counselling, advice and information.

Although adopters have the right to request an assessment of their needs for support services, there is no equivalent right to provision of support. The local authority will decide what support, if any, to provide to the individual making an application based on the assessment of need and resources that are available.

Whose responsibility is it to provide support?

The first three years

Assessing and providing support services remains the responsibility of the local authority that placed the child, for the first three years after the adoption order. (This applies outside Northern Ireland.) This includes responsibility for managing and supporting contact arrangements.

After three years

After three years, the local authority where the family lives takes over responsibility for assessing and providing support services. However, the placing authority remains responsible for supporting any contact arrangements. (If the placing authority has provided financial support during the first three years, it will also continue to be responsible for this.)

Local authorities may also – at their discretion – provide services to people outside their area when they consider it appropriate.

When children are placed with adopters through a voluntary adoption agency (VAA), they are placed with adopters in the area where the VAA operates, so a range of services will be available via the VAA, in addition to those provided by the local authority where they live. The VAA may also help to negotiate with the local authority for other services the adopters need.

Providing support

Adoptive parents have sometimes taken on damaged and disturbed children on the assumption that there would be no contact with the child's birth family until he is an adult. They adopted at a time when no one had heard of Facebook. They didn't expect their child to be able to find, or be found by, his birth parents on the strength of a few minutes at the computer. They didn't sign up for this.

Where young people are at risk and adoptive families are struggling with the complex and challenging situations that arise from unregulated contact, they need and deserve all the help professionals can give and these situations fall within the remit of adoption support services.

What can social workers do?

Many adoptive parents would like to see local authorities and agencies taking a more proactive role in stepping in when there are problems with birth parents and Facebook.

> *I feel the local authority need to make some policy decisions on this and perhaps instead of the adoptive parents monitoring and forcing this issue, they should look to be the monitors. Perhaps policy could even somehow make it illegal to make contact beyond the "contact agreement" without the prior written agreement of the adoptive parents? We really are at a loss on how to handle this ourselves, but we know we cannot be the instigators here – it has to come from an "authoritative" place.*
>
> AN ADOPTIVE PARENT

Others understandably don't want to get involved with the agency all over again. They prefer to try to deal with it on their own. Particularly where children are over 16, many of these situations are likely to occur "off the radar" of the agency.

BAAF and local authorities have begun to discuss and address the issues of social networking in adoption. Hopefully the profession will develop guidance and policies as people develop experience in this emerging area of practice.

A social worker can write a letter to a birth parent to tell them that Facebook contact is unacceptable as it is outside the original contact agreement. But of course there are limits to how much they can influence people's behaviour - and this includes adoptive parents, adopted children and teenagers, birth parents and other relatives. Some young people are determined to continue the contact by whatever means they can; and birth parents are not always prepared to listen to the views of social workers.

> *Sometimes adopters think we have more power than we have. They have to understand that we social workers don't have magic wands – we can't make birth parents not respond. We can only support people if they are prepared to be supported.*
>
> AN ADOPTION SUPPORT WORKER

In spite of these limitations, social workers can still provide invaluable help and support to families.

CASE STUDY

Our eldest adopted child is 16 and we found out a few weeks ago that she had made contact with her birth family via Facebook. They replied to her and they exchanged many emails and texts even though they know there should not be contact until she's 18. This is a huge worry for many reasons. Her birth dad is a very violent man, who now has information about us. We also adopted her two younger siblings, so this also puts them in potential danger and would cause huge emotional problems if they find out.

It has caused huge emotional upheaval for our daughter – it was really easy to make contact with them, but because she'd done it in secret, she had no support to deal with the issues it has raised, until we found out.

It is very easy for birth families to say nice things and "reinvent" the past via emails and texts, leaving a very confused 16-year-old who blamed us for everything going wrong in her life.

We are lucky that our adoption agency has been a huge help in dealing with the situation. They advised limiting opportunities for "unsafe" contact in the short term by blocking Facebook from our computer and confiscating her phone – we had already done that. A post-adoption support worker visited us and spelt out very clearly but kindly to our daughter why such contact is really unsafe both emotionally and physically, for her and the whole family.

After checking with us, he has said that he could arrange for a supervised contact session or to write and find out any information she would like from them – she's thinking about this.

Our agency have contacted the placing agency, who are planning to visit birth mum. We are pushing hard for them to do the same with birth dad – he has moved to a different area, which makes this more difficult.

Can you hold Facebook to account?

If a child is under 13 and has a Facebook account, notify Facebook – it undertakes to delete accounts of children under 13.

Many adoptive parents have found it difficult to get Facebook to act over issues to do with contact when the child is a willing party to it.

We put the following (true) scenario to Facebook:

Adoptive parents who contacted Facebook to ask to have their 15-year-old daughter's birth mother's Facebook account closed because of unregulated contact with their daughter have been told that, as it was their daughter who was contacted (rather than themselves), they are not entitled to make a complaint. They are told that such complaints can only be made by the individual who is the recipient of the messages.

A spokeswoman for Facebook in the UK confirmed that this is indeed the case, unless there is police involvement:

We provide extensive privacy settings that allow people to...block individuals with whom they wish to have no contact. This prevents those people from accessing their profile or communicating with them through Facebook. Only the account owner can choose the settings that are right for him or her. Facebook does not make these decisions on people's behalf.

If there is any inappropriate content on a page, we will respond whoever the request comes from. If it is a case of contact, we would respond if this is being dealt with by law enforcement agencies. If the police are not involved, then it is very difficult for us to do anything. If a user is not doing anything against our terms and conditions, then there's nothing that Facebook as a company can do about it.

Can anyone stop this unauthorised contact?

Some adoptive parents expect the agency to be able to stop all unmediated contact. They feel unsupported if social workers either can't stop all contact or advise a pragmatic approach which means allowing it to continue, albeit with some monitoring if possible.

The idea of controlled contact is ridiculous. Having met my child's birth mother, I can see why the courts recommended no contact apart from letters. It seems to me that courts don't remove children permanently from their families unless they are at risk, so to then suggest contact during the teen years when they are so vulnerable is very dangerous indeed.

AN ADOPTIVE PARENT

Local authorities are becoming more aware of the problem but also aware of the fact that they can't do much about it. They haven't got any power.

A LAWYER WHO SPECIALISES IN ADOPTION

Ultimately, unmediated contact is outside social workers' control, apart from arranging a court order preventing contact at the time of the adoption.

The risk of abduction

Some adoptive parents fear that their child's birth parent may try to abduct their child if he or she knows where the child lives or goes to school.

Reunite (www.reunite.org) has produced a Prevention Guide to assist parents in gathering together information relating to their child if they fear they may be abducted, as well as information which may be required in the event of an abduction. It is aimed at parents who fear their partner/ex-partner might attempt to take the child out of the country, but it would be useful for any parent who feels there is a risk that their child could be abducted.

The guide suggests that parents contact their local Child Protection Co-ordinator. It also advises that they should consider letting the following people know about the threat of abduction. Most of these people will be conversant with the procedures of local Safeguarding Boards.

If you or your child have one of the following, consider telling them what you fear, why and what you would like them to do if they see or hear anything suspicious:

- *The midwife*

- *The health visitor*

- *The family doctor*

- *The nursery officer or nursery nurse*

- *The headteacher*

- *The social worker*

- *The registered child minder*

- *The cub, scout, brownie or guide leader*

- *The youth club leader*

You may also think of others.

Remember, tell them of your fears, who can have legitimate contact with your child and, more importantly, who should not.

REUNITE CHILD ABDUCTION PREVENTION GUIDE FOR ENGLAND AND WALES

Can the police do anything?

Making contact is not in itself an offence. There may be a role for the police if:

- there was a court order for no contact;
- the child does not want the contact to continue and sees it as harassment;
- the birth relative's messages are threatening or intimidating;
- the child's birth relative has been convicted of sexual offences.

Police have a duty to protect under-16s and other people considered to be "at risk", for instance, because they have a learning disability or mental health issues.

What does the law say about children and young people who run away?

The law does not generally regard young people under the age of 16 as being able to live independently away from home.

Anyone who has care of a child without parental responsibility may do what *is reasonable* in all the circumstances to safeguard and promote the child's welfare (Children Act 1989 s3 (5) or Children (Scotland) Act 1995 s5 (1)) or Article 6 of the Children (Northern Ireland) Order 1995. It is likely to be "reasonable" to inform the police, or children's services departments, and, if appropriate, their parents, of the child/young person's safety and whereabouts.

Anyone who "takes or detains" a runaway under 16 without lawful authority may be prosecuted under s2 of the Child Abduction Act 1984 or ss83 and 89 of the Children (Scotland) Act 1995 or Article 70 (5 and 6) of the Children (Northern Ireland) Order 1995. Enforcement might be problematic, however, if the young person has chosen to stay with another adult of his or her own free will.

How the police can deal with it

Several police forces across the country are using "harbouring legislation" (Section 2 of the Child Abduction Act 1984 or section 49 of the Children Act 1989 if under 18 years and in local authority care) to tackle incidences where young people run away or go missing and are found with people considered to be inappropriate, for example, because they are much older or they encourage the young person to stay away from their home. It has been particularly useful for young people who are thought to be at risk of sexual exploitation. (In this situation, the young person will often say they are content to be in the company of the person in question.)

Leicestershire Constabulary is one of the police forces successfully using the legislation in this way and, along with the Crown Prosecution Service, have produced a protocol which describes the approach to be used. The aim is to disrupt the relationship in the first instance, thereby reducing the risks that the young person may be exposed to. In the longer term, it aims to reduce repeat incidences of children going missing from home and care.

Sixteen- and 17-year-olds can choose to leave home. If an under-18 goes missing from home, the police may actively look for them if they consider the person to be vulnerable.

They will carry out a risk assessment and decide what action (if any) to take on the basis of this. It is difficult to force young people to come home if the police do not consider them to be in danger.

If a younger child leaves home to be with a birth parent, this could be considered abduction and it may be possible to use the Child Abduction Act (as outlined above) to get them back.

Most adoptive families would avoid involving the police if at all possible. But of course, if they believe their child is in immediate danger of being abducted, they should be advised to contact the police.

> *A 16-year-old girl had run away from her adoptive home to live with her birth parents. The adoptive parents called in the police. The police visited the girl at the birth parents' home to assess the situation and do what is known as a "safe and well" check. Because she was over 16, was found to be safe and well, was not being held against her will and didn't want to come home, the police could do nothing more.*
>
> SPOKESWOMAN FROM CEOP, CHILD EXPLOITATION AND ONLINE PROTECTION CENTRE

Child Exploitation and Online Protection Centre (CEOP)

CEOP is a Government enforcement agency and has policing powers. It can take action if a case involving the internet meets its threshold of "likelihood of significant harm" – in other words, it doesn't have to wait for evidence that a crime has been committed.

When it is suspected that "grooming" (including by a parent who is a sex offender) is taking place online, CEOP can covertly monitor the online communication and trace the perpetrator. It can then pass the details to the local police force, which will be able to arrest him. Based on the level of risk, in certain cases CEOP can apply to Facebook to access someone's personal data.

Parents and children's services can contact the police or CEOP when they feel a child is at serious risk from his or her online contact.

Can you go to court to stop Facebook and other forms of contact?

In some cases, adoptive parents go to court to try to resolve situations where there is unmediated contact.

- Contact agreements made at the time of an adoption are usually voluntary and not legally binding. If the agreement was voluntary, making contact is not illegal.

- Courts are reluctant to make contact orders at the time of an adoption hearing, as that would limit the adopter's parental responsibility and ability to change the contact arrangements. Adopters need to be able to make decisions about what is in their child's best interests and this can change over time.

- Contact agreements cannot be enforced by law. This applies whether either (a) the adopters or (b) the birth parents either (a) do something that is not in the agreement or (b) fail to do something that is in the agreement.

CASE STUDY

Recently we had a case where we had applied for placement orders to progress adoption plans for two older children in foster care where the foster carer had been approved and matched as adopter. The birth father had been having direct but supervised contact but during this time mobile phone numbers were exchanged. There then followed a deluge of text messaging leading to Facebook and other email communication and very rapidly the plan for adoption became a non-starter for the older boy. One of the difficulties was the use of this communication for all sorts of promises.

At the initial hearing the high court judge took the view that 'it's a free world and they can text as much as they like'. In a subsequent hearing with a different judge, we were able to obtain an order under s.34(4) (of the Children Act 1989) which limited text messaging to one hour per day. I know even this sounds a huge amount but believe me it is nothing compared to what was going on.

Section 34(4) of the Children Act 1989 refers to children in the care of the local authority. It states:

> On an application made by the authority or the child, the court may make an order authorising the authority to refuse to allow contact between the child and any person who is mentioned in paragraphs (a) to (d) of subsection (1) (which includes parents and guardians) and is named in the order.

However, this applies only to *looked after children.*

There is a similar provision in Sections 58 (1) and 17(1)c of the Children (Scotland) Act 1995, and Article 53 in the Children (Northern Ireland) Order 1995.

Once children are adopted, any legal action has to be instigated by the adoptive parents. But in most cases, this is not a helpful route to go down.

One possible legal route is a Section 8 Prohibited Steps Order under the Children Act 1989, or a Section 11 Order under the Children (Scotland) Act 1995 or under the Children (Northern Ireland) Order 1995. This is a court order which is usually used in disputes between parents – for instance, to say that one parent may not take the child to see a grandfather who is a sex offender, or may not remove the child from the country.

When it is obvious at the time of the adoption that the birth parents are going to try to get in contact with the child, or if there is trouble between the placement and the adoption order going through, a local authority might suggest taking out a Prohibited Steps Order before the adoption is finalised. The local authority might be prepared to fund this, either at the time or later if it proves necessary.

Once the adoption has gone through, the adoptive parents have parental responsibility for the child. So if they want to take legal action against a birth parent who is contacting the child, it must be the adoptive parents – rather than the local authority – who take the matter to court.

However, this does not happen very often. The court will take into account the child's own wishes, so the chances of success largely depend on whether he wants the contact or not. If he does want it, the chances of getting a court order against the birth parent are slim.

Another possibility is a court injunction, under the Family Law Act 1996, designed to prevent someone from pestering or harassing another person. This is an option if, for example, the child is being repeatedly contacted or followed by a birth parent. The adoptive parents can use the Family Law Act 1996 because they have been part of the same family proceedings (adoption) with the birth parents. If they or their child have been threatened or distressed by contact from the birth parent or another member of the birth family, they could apply for an order under the Protection from Harassment Act 1997. In Scotland, the Family Law (Scotland) Act 2006 and, in Northern Ireland, the Protection from Harassment Order 1997, offer similar possibilities.

Again, the child's or young person's own wishes and feelings will be taken into account. It may be hard to get a court to accept that unregulated contact is damaging to the child's welfare if the child wants or welcomes the contact with the birth parent (even if others feel that it is damaging). Even if the child is as young as 11 or 12, the court would want to know what the child thinks. If the child says they want to have the contact, the adoptive parents are unlikely to be able to achieve anything this way.

In most cases, adoptive parents decide against going down the route of taking their child's birth parents to court because:

- it feels like a heavy-handed approach and ratchets up the emotional tension;
- it brings them into direct conflict with the birth parents, which could be hard for the child to cope with;
- it could involve disclosing the child's name and address.

It also involves significant costs. You could approach the Legal Services Commission (in England and Wales) or the Scottish Legal Aid, or Northern Ireland Legal Services Commission, to find out whether or not they could help with funding such a case, and/or supporting affected families in some way. Local authorities may be prepared to consider funding it as part of adoption support.

Peer support for adoptive parents

Adoptive parents can be a huge help to each other in many ways – offering and exchanging information, practical suggestions, understanding and moral support. Some local authorities and adoption agencies run support groups and training courses where adoptive parents can meet with others and discuss their experiences.

And then – of course – there's the internet. Adoption UK (www.adoptionuk.org.uk) has a website with a messageboard where adoptive parents can post messages, anonymously, to share their experiences with others and ask or offer advice. Adoptive families facing Facebook dilemmas and traumas are helping one another to get through.

> *I've just joined the message board on Adoption UK – it makes me realise why the kids use Facebook!*
>
> A SPECIAL GUARDIAN

Surviving the crisis

> *My view, formed over the course of five years in this role, is that too many children with very disturbed or non-existent attachments are now being placed for adoption. Whilst it is, of course, the case that these children need to be cared for in some way, matching them with adoptive parents who are trying to replace the birth child they were unable to have themselves, and of whom they have dreamt for many years, can be worse for the child than never having his or her own "forever family", and worse for the adopter than never having a child they can call their own.*
>
> AN ADOPTION SUPPORT WORKER

Even when adopted children and young people do not have attachment problems and have successfully formed attachments to their adoptive families, there is sometimes a period of rebellion and conflict in adolescence. And – as we have seen – when a young person is having unmediated contact with birth relatives, it can compound this, resulting in a family crisis.

Sometimes young people talk about going off to live with their birth parents and adoptive parents feel they can't get through to them. There is likely to be a period of intense stress, distress and arguments. If a young person leaves home for a short time and then returns, it is unlikely to be a happy situation for anyone. The relationship between the young person and their adoptive parents will have taken a hammering and everyone will be feeling raw.

CASE STUDY

Our daughter came to us at the age of six after having suffered sexual abuse in her family. We have had a huge amount of trouble with birth parents contacting her as soon as she turned 16 last year. I still don't know if she found them or if her mother found her. Our daughter told us she was going to stay with friends but she was at her birth mother's house for three nights. The father is a Schedule 1 offender and both parents have personality disorders. The mother abuses drugs and alcohol and has had more children since, and has been allowed to keep them. There seems to be something that pulls her to her mother. Perhaps she is afraid the younger children are not being looked after properly.

It has been a living hell for months and has nearly broken down the placement. We are getting support – a "team around the child", once a month – but all the police and post-adoption service will say is that, because she's over 16, there's nothing they can do. But emotionally she is functioning at the level of about 12. I can't understand why they can't protect her.

The companies running the social networking sites don't care – I haven't even been able to contact Facebook to get her details taken down.

I know all the research about contact and I know kids need contact, but this woman refuses to come to social services to have contact. Maybe with less complex cases than my daughter's, it might be possible to prevent some of this by preparing children for contact and going through everything with them. But my daughter has been so damaged by what happened to her that she was never, ever able to attach to us. I am interested in why the authorities seem powerless to police this area.

An adoptive mother

Encourage parents to keep the lines of communication open any way they can, even if this has to be by texts and phone calls. Making sure the young person has a mobile phone and keeping the credits topped up are critical for keeping communication going when a young person leaves home for short or long periods of time.

When young people get into a cycle of going to their birth parents and then coming home, adoptive parents sometimes feel the situation is untenable. They may be driven to desperation and feel ready to give up on a young person who repeatedly runs away. The young person may want to go and live with the birth parent. But of course if the birth parent represents a risk, social workers will need to encourage the young person to look for an alternative way to live independently if the adoption breaks down.

> *Adoptive mum is saying: 'If he wants to go and live with them so badly, he can go'. I am having to tell the child and the adoptive mum quite firmly: 'That's not an option'.*
>
> AN ADOPTION SUPPORT WORKER

The long-term outcome can be positive

When an adoption breaks down, the adoptive family are likely to feel traumatised, guilty and bereft. They will need time, help and support to get through this. However bad things get, try to hold out some hope for a more positive outcome in the longer term.

A study by David Howe (1996) of the University of East Anglia showed that many adoptive parents eventually enjoy a more intense, caring and reciprocal relationship with their adoptive child than they would ever have thought possible during their child's difficult and demanding teenage years.

Researchers asked adopters about their current relationships with their grown-up adopted children and the relationships they had with them during adolescence. The study covered 100 adopted people who were at least 23 years old.

Howe categorised the children into three groups, according to the type of care they had experienced before their placement. He asked parents what their children had been like as teenagers. There were ten measures of adolescent problem behaviour (self-mutilation, eating disorder, lying, truancy, exclusion from school, running away from home, substance abuse, theft from home, offences outside the home and violence against a family member).

At the time of the study, by which time the children were all young adults, 93 per cent of parents reviewed the adoption positively and said relationships with their child were good. The biggest improvement was found in the group of children who had had adverse experiences in early life and were adopted relatively late, i.e. after babyhood. Although some of these children had problem behaviours throughout their childhood, adolescence was a time when their angry and challenging behaviour tried their parents to the limit. In this group, only 38 per cent of parents felt that relationships with their child had been positive in adolescence; but 67 per cent reported their current relationship was positive.

Those who did manage to ride the storm (which could last several years) often found that their very insecure, hostile and angry children slowly began to develop an increased sense of security and self-confidence. They stopped fighting their parents and during their 20s, seemingly for the first time, were able to accept their love without feeling confused, angry and anxious.

In a few cases, relationships did not recover and parents and children had lost contact or conflict continued (although the longer term outcome could still improve for this group as well – the research only followed them up to a certain point in time).

Coming out the other side

The two examples below show that, in some cases, if the situation is managed well, even contact initiated via Facebook can prove beneficial once the dust has settled.

CASE STUDY

A 14-year-old girl made Facebook contact with a maternal aunt. Unbeknown to her adoptive parents, the girl went to meet her aunt and cousin. Her aunt "treated" her to a tattoo. Her parents were very distressed about this.

I met with them and their daughter and we thought of two ways forward. One was that I would contact and try to meet with the aunt. The other was that I would write a history for the adopted girl who wanted more information about her background than her life story book gave. The aunt agreed to meet me and was contrite. She was keen to have contact and clear that this would be on the adopters' terms. She and her daughter have since met for a meal with the adoptive family and this went well. The adoptive parents feel that their daughter has been more settled since then. Coming to discuss her story had filled in some gaps and contact with her aunt is currently proving positive.

I was hugely impressed by the maturity and generosity of the adoptive parents who realistically decided that once the contact had been made it could not be unmade and it was better for them to become involved and manage it than to alienate the aunt and possibly their own daughter.

An adoption support worker

CASE STUDY

I was contacted by a couple whose 13-year-old adopted daughter had contacted her birth mother on Facebook without letting them know. The birth mother had been 16 when she gave birth and had never told her parents or her siblings of her baby's existence. Fortunately she dealt with the issue very well. She asked the child if her parents knew what she was doing. The child lied and said they did. The birth mother said she was not happy about this way of making contact and would get in touch with children's services. The child then told her mum what she had done.

The birth mother met with her local post-adoption worker. She was very distressed that her family might find out about the child. She had turned her life around, gone to university and is now married with two young children.

We have now established annual letterbox contact and the adopted girl is very happy with this. We have been very clear that this cannot be taken further until she is over 18.

An adoption support worker

When things are at their worst, try to encourage adopters not to give up hope. Things do change – young people mature and see things differently, people adjust and come to terms with events, and even seemingly disastrous situations can turn around in time.

Our daughter is returning to her practical self and has a college interview next week, so hopefully a year of chaos and instability is now behind us.

AN ADOPTIVE MOTHER

Things are very good for my daughter…we have put a lot of work into supporting her and trying to draw her back into the family after some nightmare years…so far so good…and we love her to smithereens…that's all we have left after being brought very low over a long period of time… the love.

AN ADOPTIVE MOTHER

Unhappy young people have always run away from home. Children can sometimes drift into the underworld, but there may be something in them that will bring them out. Sometimes they come back in their 20s and acknowledge the value of what adopters gave them in their childhood. Adolescence can be so explosive…but it's not the end.

AN ADOPTION SOCIAL WORKER

In the following case, Katie, now 16, and who was given up for adoption at the age of 6 months by her birth parents, who did not want to keep her, shares her experience. This is what she says.

CASE STUDY

One day, when I was 14, I found my birth certificate. I used the internet to trace my birth grandparents' address. I wrote to them and my birth father rang me a few days later. I was so excited at first. He made himself seem like a lovely father.

At first it was all 'How are you, my darling daughter?' but the next time it would be abuse and foul language. He would phone every night when he was drunk and rant at me. My birth father is not a nice guy. He and one of my birth sisters send abusive messages to me on Facebook. My birth sister used to email me every day, saying I was dirt and I should die. They try to manipulate me by telling me things that aren't true. Once he put my birth mother on the phone but I could tell she was being forced to talk to me. I was desperate for them to like me even when they rejected me and treated me like dirt. My birth parents had told everyone in the family that I was dead.

I didn't tell my mum for about two months. I was stressed out and throwing up all the time. I don't like lying to my mum. But I wouldn't have wanted to approach her [to find out about the birth family] because I wouldn't have wanted to hurt her feelings.

Once my birth father said to me 'I know everything that's going on in your life. I've got Facebook right here in front of me' and he started reading from my profile and my mum's profile. It's like stalking – he uses other people's accounts to make contact.

When they ring it destroys me a little bit. But they don't do it that often now. If I hadn't contacted them, I would have lived my life wondering – but now I know the brutal reality. It stops me from ever wanting to know them.

Katie's mum adds:

Katie's birth relatives didn't want contact after the adoption. We had told Katie about her history as she was growing up.

When this contact happened, we went through the history again with Katie but at first she didn't want to believe it. She said: 'That can't be right – you've got it wrong'.

At first we were in a state of panic. We didn't know if they'd turn up here or what they might do to us. While all of this was going on, Katie struggled a lot with all aspects of her life. For a long time I didn't know where to turn for help and I felt incredibly frustrated.

It's my view now that they will always be there. They are part of Katie's life and she has to find a way of coping with it as best she can. It's really hard for Katie and for us but that's how it's got to be.

Katie has had some life story work and counselling from an adoption support worker from the local authority adoption support service. She has also been advised about stopping this damaging contact and involving the police, but – for the moment at least – she is choosing not to put an end to the contact. And, as her mother points out, she can be very determined.

Some months after Katie first made contact with her extended birth family, Katie's eldest birth sister, who had left home and moved to a refuge at the age of 15 several years ago, also made contact with Katie through Facebook. The following day, Katie got on a train (without telling her parents at first) and went to the town where she lives, to meet her. Something positive has come out of all the stress and anguish. The two sisters have re-connected and forged a firm friendship, and Katie's adoptive parents can see that this is important to both of them.

Looking ahead

Adoption workers are facing up to Facebook and are finding new ways to support adopted children, adopters and birth families through the situations that arise through social networking.

This book has looked at how they are doing this and what they need to consider in their day-to-day work.

There are wider questions, as yet unanswered, about the impact of the revolution in social networking on adoption:

- Will it be possible, in the years to come, to keep a child's identity secret?

- If not, will "closed" adoptions become a thing of the past?

- What would be the implications for children and their adoptive families?

- We already ask a huge amount from adoptive parents who take on children from traumatic backgrounds. If prospective adopters were asked to expect and accept face-to-face contact with the child's birth family during his or her childhood, would anyone still be willing to adopt?

- Does all of this spell the beginning of the end of adoption in the UK as we now know it?

We can't tell, right now, exactly how all of this will unfold or where it will take us. But one thing is certain – a new reality is emerging, which will affect everyone who is involved in or touched by adoption.

Appendix 1
Privacy settings on Facebook

To get to this section, click on "Account" in the top right-hand corner of your profile page and select "Privacy settings".

This section controls who can see all the content you post on a day-to-day basis (such as status updates, photos and videos). It also includes some things you share about yourself (birthday and contact information) and content others share about you (comments on your posts and photos and videos you've been tagged in). You can set these with one click, and your settings will apply to all the day-to-day content you post in the future. "Customise settings" displays a full list so you can control the privacy level for each setting.

Facebook makes certain information visible to everyone because it wants other people to be able to find and connect with you on Facebook.

- Name and profile picture are visible to everyone so real-world friends can recognise you. These are also displayed when you write on someone's wall.
- Gender is public.
- Networks are visible to everyone so you can see who else is part of your network (and will have access to your information) if you choose "Friends and Networks" for any of your privacy settings.

Other information in this section, including hometown and interests, is visible by default so others will be able to see it unless you change the settings.

This section controls what information is shared with websites and applications, including search engines (applications and websites you and your friends use already have access to your name, profile picture, gender, networks, friend list, user ID, and any other information you share with everyone). When your friends use certain applications and games, this can make some of your information available to others – if you don't want this to happen, use the settings to change it. If you don't want people to be able to find you by using a search engine outside Facebook (e.g. Google), make sure the box 'Enable public search' is not ticked.

The default privacy settings make quite a lot of your information visible to "everyone". You need to change the settings if you want to make your information more private.

103

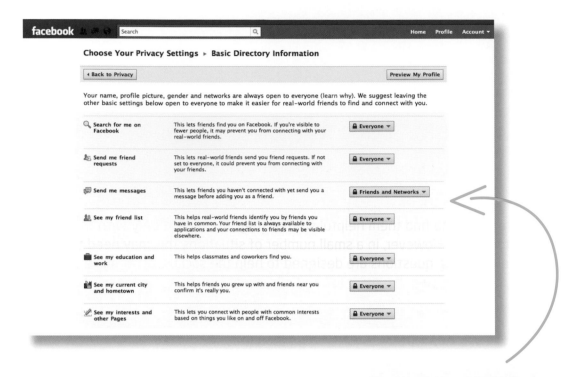

If you are not happy with these default settings, you must change them.

You can get more information about this from *A guide to protecting your privacy on Facebook* on www.bbc.co.uk.

Appendix 2
An example of a risk assessment for the use of photographs in information exchange (letterbox) services

When children are placed for adoption, it is usual for there to be an exchange of information between the adoptive family and birth family via a third party. Photographs are often included in this exchange; photographs can help birth family members to move on, and children can also find them helpful so that they are not left only with the image in their life story book. However, in a small number of situations this may need to be assessed. The following questions are designed to help the social worker make a risk assessment. This is not an exhaustive list and additional questions can be added based on the circumstances in each case.

The responses need to be analysed by balancing the positives and negatives. Remember that some issues will be more significant than others.

Name of child/ren to be placed for adoption..

Name and relationship of birth family member (answer each question in relation to them as an individual, use separate sheet for each person)..

	Evidence
Are they in support of the plan for adoption?	
Is there evidence that they have co-operated with children's services?	
Is there any evidence that they have caused concerns for the foster carer, e.g. turning up unannounced, threats, etc?	
Have they ever expressed the view that they will try to trace the child once placed for adoption?	
Have they ever been accused or convicted of offences against children?	
Do they mix with people who have been accused of or have been convicted of offences against children?	
Do you think they will share any photos with others? If so, who?	
Are they in prison? What are the implications of this?	

	Evidence
Is the child/ren going to be placed geographically close to the birth family?	
Is the child very recognisable/distinguishing features?	
Do they already participate in an information exchange for another child/ren? If so, is it appropriate?	
Is there any other family member who is going to have "letterbox" with photos who may share them with this person?	
Do they have computer skills?	
Do they have a Facebook or other social network site?	
If they have met the prospective adopters, was this positive?	
Is there any evidence of previous misuse or inappropriate use of photographs?	
Might they be unduly distressed or their mental health affected by receiving photos?	
Are there any other issues to be concerned about, e.g. violence, intimidation/threat?	
What is the child's view?	
What is the view of the prospective adoptive parent(s) (if available)?	

Analysis
Conclusion

Signed ....

Name & position ....

Date...

This draft agreement has been reproduced with kind permission of Berkshire Adoption Advisory Service and SEPAN (South East Post Adoption Network) Contact Group.

Appendix 3
An example of a virtual contact centre that allows safe and secure email contact

Dads' Space 1-2-1 is a secure online communication service or "virtual contact centre" which provides a safe way for separated parents to stay in contact with their children.

Designed primarily for child contact issues after separation due to domestic violence and allegations of abuse, this service can also be used where parents are separated from their children who are in foster care or adoptive families, or where siblings are separated in the care system.

The service was developed to provide a means of contact that works for children and allows non-resident parents to communicate with their children in a way that does not place either the child or other parent(s) at risk. It acts as a risk management strategy for any agency organising contact for families with high risk issues.

How does Dads' Space work?

Like child contact in the real world, there are levels of access depending on safety and risk. Professionals refer families and complete a risk assessment. Depending on the risk assessment, the child and their parent will be allowed contact at one of two levels:

Supervised – this level allows a broad exchange of information, sharing photos and playing games. However, all communication is moderated (checked) before it is transmitted.

Supported – this allows free real-time communication in which messages are randomly checked after being sent to ensure that the service is being used appropriately.

Who can use it?

At the time of writing, Dads' Space 1-2-1 is open to new referrals from adoption social workers working with families for whom this service could be helpful, whether or not domestic violence was a feature in the child's birth family. Mothers and fathers as well as siblings can be referred.

This service could be helpful in a proportion of adoption cases in which there are concerns about a child or young person who is having social networking contact with a birth relative or where such contact seems imminent. If birth relatives have requested contact or have tried to establish contact via Facebook and it has been discussed and agreed that online contact can take place, this kind of secure online service could be helpful in some cases. It provides a channel for online contact without compromising the child's or young person's identity and contact details or opening up all the information on their Facebook page to the birth relative (and vice versa). It also allows the contact to be screened by a moderator who is alert to potential risks and can pick up on any inappropriate questions or language. For instance, if a birth parent asked the child for their mobile phone number, the moderator can pick this up, ensure the message is not sent, and discuss it with the parent. High risk emails are not approved for sending and the appropriate authorities are notified of any such incidents. This provides some reassurance for the adoptive family.

There are benefits in having a third party, rather than the adoptive parent, moderate the content. It allows the child or young person to communicate with their birth relative without feeling that their privacy is being invaded by their adoptive parents monitoring the messages themselves.

Dads' Space 1-2-1 is a relatively low-cost service, even compared to letterbox contact. It can be used with children from four years upwards.

This service could provide a model for similar web-based communication systems to allow safe email contact in adoption.

Who manages this service?

It is managed by Respect, the national association for professionals working with people to end their abusive behaviour, and developed in partnership with Atticmedia. Respect also works with Atticmedia on Dads' Space, a website which provides entertaining parenting advice for all fathers as well as addressing more complex issues of domestic violence and post-separation parenting. Dads' Space 1-2-1 was set up in 2008. It has been funded so far by the (former) Department for Children, Schools and Families, and its funding is secure until October 2010 when it is hoped other sources of funding will be forthcoming.

For more information or to find out how to make a referral, visit www.respect.uk.net (see 'Professionals referring to Dads' Space 1-2-1').

References

BAAF (1999) *Contact in Permanent Placement: Guidance for local authorities in England and Wales and Scotland*, London: BAAF

Brodzinsky D, Schechter M and Marantz Henig R, *A Psychosocial Model of Adoption Adjustment*, www.americanadoptioncongress.org/grief_brodzinsky_article.php

Brodzinsky D, Smith D and Brodzinsky A (1998) *Children's Adjustment to Adoption: Developmental and clinical issues*, London: Sage

Childnet report: *Young People and Social Networking Services: A Childnet International Research Report* (see the full report at www.digizen.org)

CHIS (Children's Charities Coalition on Internet Safety (2009) *Digital Manifesto*

Cullen D (2007) 'Confidentiality in adoption: local authority's negligence in disclosing name and whereabouts of adopters to birth family', *Adoption & Fostering*, 31:1, pp. 123-124

Howe D (1996) 'Adopters' relationships with their adopted children from adolescence to early adulthood', *Adoption & Fostering*, 20:5, 1996, pp 35-43

Kaniuk J (2010) *Ten Top Tips for Supporting Adopters*, London: BAAF

Neil E (2002) 'Managing face-to-face contact for young adopted children', in Argent H (ed) *Staying Connected*, London: BAAF

Neil E *et al* (2010) *Helping Birth Families*, London: BAAF, http://www.adoptionresearchinitiative.org.uk/exec/summary5a.pdf

Ofcom Media Literacy Audit 2009: www.ofcom.org.uk/advice/media_literacy/medlitpub/medlitpubrss/uk_childrens_ml

Reunite Child Abduction Prevention Guide for England and Wales http://www.reunite.org/edit/files/Prevention%20Guide%20E&W.pdf

I am following my birth father on Facebook, an account published in The Guardian, 30.07.09.

Schofield G (2009) 'Parenting while apart: the experiences of birth parents of children in long-term foster care': Full Research Report ESRC End of Award Report, RES-000-22-2606. Swindon: ESRC

The Futures Company/YouthNet Survey 2009, www.youthnet.org/mediaandcampaigns/pressreleases/hybrid-lives

UK Council for Child Internet Safety (2009) *Click Clever, Click Safe: The first UK child internet safety strategy*, UK Council for Child Internet Safety

Williams R (2010) 'You worry about their personal safety', *Society Guardian*, 24 March 2010

Verrier N (2010) *Coming Home to Self: Healing the primal wound*, London: BAAF

Finding out more

There is a huge amount of information available about the general issue of safety on the internet, so that people have the skills, knowledge and understanding to help children and young people to stay safe online.

Advice/information about safety on the internet

Child Exploitation and Online Protection Centre: www.ceop.gov.uk

CEOP provides an internet safety programme for children and young people, called Thinkuknow: **www.thinkuknow.co.uk**

Many websites used by children and young people incorporate the CEOP "panic button" which allows them to report unacceptable online behaviour by adults, e.g. online grooming by paedophiles. (At the time of writing, Facebook does not incorporate the CEOP panic button on the site.)

Childnet: www.childnet.com

Childnet has produced the CD-ROM *KnowIT All for Parents* (visit www.childnet-int.org/kia) to help parents make sure their child uses the internet safely. It also produces a leaflet for parents and young people on social networking sites, and has resources in Hindi, Punjabi and Urdu.

MyGuide: www.myguide.gov.uk

This is a Government-run online training resource for adults to learn about the internet.

GetNetWise:www.getnetwise.org

This website has a list of internet safety tools for families, with explanations about what each one can do in terms of monitoring, filtering and blocking. For instance, there are various products which will monitor a child's internet use, either with or without his or her knowledge. The website also provides how-to video tutorials, e.g. on setting privacy settings.

www.sophos.com

This website provides lots of useful information about security on the internet.

Ofcom: www.ofcom.org.uk/advice/guides/media

The Ofcom website provides a guide for parents and carers on how to use parental controls and filters to manage children's access to digital TV and internet content.

Ofcom: www.ofcom.org.uk/files/2009/10/location.pdf

A link to Ofcom's guide for parents on how to keep children safe when using location-based services with mobile phones.

Vodafone: http://parents.vodafone.com/ locationservices

This is a link to Vodafone's parents' guide to location services.

Internet Watch Foundation: www.iwf.org.uk

This website enables internet users to report online child pornography.

Get Safe Online: www.getsafeonline.org

A joint initiative between the Government, law enforcement and the business and public sectors, which provides free, independent, user-friendly advice about using the internet safely.

NSPCC/Sport England: www.nspcc.org.uk/Inform/cpsu/Resources/Briefings/ briefings_wda60650.html

Guidance produced jointly by NSPCC and Sport England for sports clubs and sport governing bodies that gives advice on the use of photographs of children and also how to use social networking and other websites safely.

Reunite: www.reunite.org

Reunite produces a guide on what to do if you fear your child is at risk of abduction. The guide mostly concerns international abduction but has useful information for anyone afraid of their child being abducted. The guide can be seen at: www.reunite.org/edit/ files/Prevention%20Guide%20E&W.pdf.

Advice/information about adoption, contact and reunion

BAAF

Head Office
Saffron House
6-10 Kirby Street
London
EC1N 8TS
Tel: 020 7421 2600
www.baaf.org.uk
BAAF Cymru: Tel 029 2076 1155
BAAF Northern Ireland: Tel 028 9031 5494
BAAF Scotland: Tel 0131 226 9270

BAAF also operates www.adoptionresearchreunion.org.uk

Adoption UK

Linden House
55 The Green
South Bar Street
Banbury OX16 9AB
Tel: 01295 752240
www.adoptionuk.org.uk
Adoption UK has a number of regional offices throughout the UK.

Supporting adults affected by adoption - NORCAP

112 Church Road
Wheatley
Oxfordshire OX33 1LU
Tel: 01865 875000
www.norcap.org.uk

Adoption contact registers

The Adoption Contact Register

Room C202, General Register Office
Trafalgar Road
Southport PR8 2HH
Tel: 0151 471 4252
www.gro.gov.uk
For adoptions that took place in England and Wales

Birthlink

21 Castle Street
Edinburgh EH2 3DN
Tel: 0131 225 6441
www.birthlink.org.uk
For adoptions that took place in Scotland

General Register Office

Oxford House, 49-55 Chichester Street
Belfast BT1 4HL
Tel: 028 9151 3101
www.groni.gov.uk
For adoptions that took place in Northern Ireland

Post-adoption centres

England and Wales

All local authorities in England and Wales have an Adoption Support Adviser, who can give advice to people affected by adoption, and direct you to post-adoption centres.

Scotland and Northern Ireland

Birthlink
21 Castle Street
Edinburgh EH2 3DN
Tel: 0131 225 6441
www.birthlink.org.uk

Barnardo's Scottish Adoption Advice Services
Suite 5/3, Skypark SP5
45 Finnieston Street
Glasgow G3 8JU
Tel: 0141 248 7530
www.barnardos.org.uk/saas.htm

Adoption Routes
Ground Floor
Unit 2, 18 Heron Road
Belfast BT3 9LE
Tel: 028 90736080
www.adoptionroutes.co.uk

Family Care Society
511 Ormeau Road
Belfast BT7 3GS
Tel: 028 90691133
www.familycaresociety.net/